My Time, My Life

A Father's Love for His Daughter Never Dies

Mario Jannatpour

Copyright © 2013 Mario Jannatpour
All rights reserved.
ISBN: 1491225599
ISBN 13: 9781491225592

Dedication

To my love: Smitha.

Acknowledgements

I enjoyed writing this book. It brought back a lot of memories of my childhood, my family, and my friends, so I have a lot of people I'd like to acknowledge.

I want to thank my amazing wife, Smitha. Every day I am reminded how grateful I am you decided to marry me.

I want to thank my two wonderful daughters, Ria and Puja. You are both the light of my life. I am happy you both like the cover of the book. Puja: no, the little girl on the cover is not you. Ria: I'm sorry you find the subtitle cheesy. I wrote this book for both of you, so when you're twenty-five years old, you will always have this book.

Thanks to my dad and mom, Kaz and Virginia. You were always there for me when I was growing up. I have great childhood memories. Thanks for all the sacrifices you made.

Thanks to my stepmom, Merelene. I am so happy you and my dad are together and that you are a part of our family.

Thanks to my two brothers, Vic and Paul, for our time together when we were growing up. We had a lot of good times together. I wish you continued happiness in your lives.

Thanks to my two cousins, Sid and John. For three years you were my brothers. I was heartbroken when you moved away. I loved having both of you in our family.

Thanks to my two beautiful sisters-in-law, Vivienne and Anusha. I am so happy for our times together.

Thanks to my two brothers-in-law, Bala and Karthik. I look forward to the next time we see each other.

Thanks to my two nephews, Gautham and Parth. I will kiss you both on your cheeks the next time I see you.

A special thanks to my mother-in-law, Sugantha. You are the best mother-in-law in the world. Thank you for all of your support of me and my career. I love your commitment to our family.

Thanks to Beatriz Blanc, my Tia Tati. I salute you in this book for saving my birthday party when I was a kid. I love you. Thanks for everything you did for us when we were young. You will always be our beautiful, hip, hot aunt.

Thanks to my cousins, Marc and Rick. We had a lot of good times growing up. I wish we had spent more time together. I do remember the summer you spent with us. We had seven boys in the house that summer. How did we survive?

Thanks to Marc and Rick's wives, Tina and Isabelle. You need to come visit us in Colorado before it's all said and done. And thanks to the next generation, my second cousins, Jeanine, Shannon, Rachel, and Dylan.

Thanks to my cousins, Monty and Courtney, who were so gracious enough to let us crash at their house for a week this past summer. We had a great time. I wrote a portion of this book at their home. Monty—I hope to get some tennis lessons soon so I will give you a better game next time.

Thanks to all my cousins: Mohsen, Mogee, Shahin, Mahin, Simin, Reza, Susan, Sima, Sudi, David, Majid, Marzie, Mark, Ali, Mo, and Hassan. And to the next generation of cousins: Mary, Jaleh, Sonny, Joe, Pete, Layla, Nina, Nedda, Evan, Jasmine, Kayvon, Z, Nicholas, Riker, Kiyan, Amir, Rana, Dustin, Zachary, Alex, Ashley, David, and Hannah. And the next generation: Brenden, Cameron, Vida and Taya. Lastly, all of the spouses, boyfriends and girlfriends of my cousins, sorry I didn't have enough room to include all of you here.

A special thank you to my cousin, Danna, for all of the love and support you gave us younger cousins when we were growing up. I love you for everything you did for the family.

I want to give a huge salute and thank you to Ryan Higgens, my editor. Ryan is great to work with. He does an amazing job turning my ramblings into coherent writing. If any of you are aspiring writers, I highly recommend you have Ryan Higgens edit your book.

Two other people I would like to thank are Joe Konrath and KM Weiland. Joe is a beacon of light and inspiration for writers. His blog is a must-read for anyone in the publishing industry. KM has great writing tips and an excellent blog that all writers need to follow. Thanks so much to both of you for the work you do in offering valuable advice to aspiring writers. I am truly grateful.

I'd like to thank a lot of my friends from my childhood days to the present. When you look back on your life, you realize what a treasure good friendships are.

All of my Chalet Woods friends: Brad, Steve, Paul, Chuck, Skip, Ellen, Arch, Vance, Stacey, Mike, Kevin, Dick, Inge, Katie, Cindy, Tracy, Jeff, and Sally. There are many more, but these are the ones I remember most from my childhood neighborhood in Virginia.

Thanks to my best friend in sixth grade, Kevin Lennox. I wish I had gotten the chance to thank Mrs. Patterson for all she did for me in sixth grade.

Thanks to Ty Murray, one of my football buddies from the SYA Warhawks. I've reconnected with Ty recently on social media. We both enjoy sending emails to each other reminiscing about the good old days and the crazy things we did.

My best friend in middle school was Neal Zarou. We had great times together. Every time I hear the Doobie Brothers sing *Black Water*, I see and hear Neal singing the song.

One of my best friends in high school was Kurt Grall. I am sorry Kurt for what I did. It was my fault that our friendship ended.

A salute and thanks to all of the people I worked with at the Applewood Pit in Boulder. A lot of us grew up there together. My brother Vic and I spent a lifetime side by side behind the grill cooking pancakes, eggs, bacon, sausage, biscuits and gravy, and all kinds of omelets. I have good memories working with my dad, mom, and my brother Paul. It was a hard life, but we made the best of it.

Thanks to Dan McKenna and his wife, Barb. Dan is one of my lifelong friends. Dan and I met right after I graduated from high school. We had great times riding our bikes, hanging out, camping, driving up to the Grand Tetons (those Pronghorn love to run!), fishing, going to concerts at Red Rocks, listening to Talking Heads, and just being together. Dan, I only wish you the best in life. Stay true to yourself. From your friend, mAr.

Thanks to Jay and Laina Albrecht. I value our friendship. I have tremendous respect for both of you and wish you tons of success and happiness with your business, family, and life.

Thanks to Greg and Amanda Jenkins. You are always there when I need help. I appreciate it.

Thanks to Gary Brenner, you made my bus rides to the DTC years ago so enjoyable as we sat together and chatted about life.

Thanks to Eric Lawson and his wife, Andreanna. Eric is a character. I keep telling him he needs to write his autobiography. How many people do you know who have their name on the Stanley Cup, played professional football in Europe, and aspire to be a grizzly bear expert? I recently made it a point to spend an afternoon visiting with Eric and Andreanna. It was just like old times.

Thank you to Christina Fiflis and David Eason for your friendship over the years. A special thank you to David. You were our knight in shining armor many years ago when we needed help. We are truly grateful.

Thanks to all my work friends over the years. A special thanks to Mike James, Steve Kowal, Ric Kuhlman, Derek Dionne, Darren Smith, Marc Bonsignore and Jeff Milum.

Thank you to Brian Burns: a friend and a mentor. We had a good run. I wish our time together working as a team had been longer.

Thanks to Paul and Susan Carlson. I enjoy our friendship; I just wish we had more time to get together.

A special thanks to Dan Johnson for giving me the opportunity to work at RE/MAX Alliance.

Thanks to Ellen Lutz for being a great colleague. I always appreciate all the help you give me. You are a true professional and a friend.

I am grateful for the leadership and management team at RE/MAX Alliance. Thank you for all of the help and encouragement you have given to me over the years: Chuck Ochsner, Chad Ochsner, Kim Hawkins, Meggan Kramer, Eric Edwards, and Mike Scott.

Many thanks to all of my real estate customers I have helped since 2002. I always tell people the best part of my job is the relationships I have made with the clients I have helped over the years.

And thank you to my good friends Heinz, Milen, Ravinder, Keani, and Alex. I look forward to our next road trip together.

Lastly, I want to thank the Boulder Bikram Yoga Studio. I started doing hot yoga earlier this year. It has changed my life: I have lost weight, I am getting cardio exercise, and the workouts are great. I have so much more energy nowadays. I want to thank some of the teachers I know best: JJ (shake out your ponytail), Brenda (I'm from Wisconsin), Luna (you are the captain of your own ship), Jonny, (keep coming every day, it's just like brushing your teeth), Paulina (it's about time), Francisco (don't get attached to the outcome, focus on the journey), Tim (move your magnificent knee), and Lori (it's all good). Namaste.

Table of Contents

One

"And once the storm is over you won't remember how you made it through, how you managed to survive. You won't even be sure, in fact, whether the storm is really over. But one thing is certain. When you come out of the storm you won't be the same person who walked in. That's what this storm's all about."
— *Haruki Murakami*

Last night was the first time I ever thought about suicide. It was just a thought, but it scared me. Why was I feeling this way? When I was young I had such high expectations for my life. I was going to do so much. I was going to be successful. I thought I would be happy. Here I was at twenty-four years old and a complete failure.

If I did kill myself the epitaph on my headstone would be brief:

Michelle Parker
Daughter of James Parker and Kayla Kumar
She came and went without anyone noticing. A life lost.

People would say:

"She looked happy. How could she do that?"

"Michelle Parker? I can't believe it. I knew her. She was so pretty. Why would she kill herself?"

"How sad, she was just twenty-four years old. What a waste."

"Didn't she realize how precious life is?"

This is my problem: I think too much, and I worry too much.

I made the last turn on my commute; I was very close to my office. My drive time lately had become another opportunity to lament about my life. The building was straight ahead. I parked my car and took a deep breath. "Let's do this! I am ready." I tried to get pumped up for work but it was no use.

* * *

I hate my job. What was the point of going to college and getting a good degree? For this? I can't take it anymore.

I was running late for the meeting. One of the big Corporate VP's had come in today from the east coast to pump us up. Friday, they felt, was the best day to rally the troops: just before the weekend. These meetings were all the same. The intimidation tactics get old fast and eventually you tune everything out. The last time one of the VP's held a meeting, she was so brutal that she made Todd Jamison, one of the sales reps, cry openly in the meeting. I felt so bad; it was so degrading for all of us.

I was frantically pounding away on my keyboard. I had to finish entering notes in my database activity program from the sales call I had just finished. I took off my headset and hung it up on the edge of my cube. I stood up and stretched my legs – wow, they were tight. I needed to get the blood flowing again. I looked out over the sea of cubes: it was empty. All of the sales reps had already gone to the meeting. I hated being late; I knew I would most likely be called out on the carpet and embarrassed in front of everyone.

As I was stretching, my cell phone vibrated on my desk. I looked at the display and tapped the answer button on my phone, "Hi Mom."

"Hi Champ, are you busy?" she said.

"Yes. What is it?" I hated when she called me that.

"I don't know. I just called to see how my Champ is doing."

"I told you not to call me that anymore. That was eight years ago. I gave all that up."

"You'll always be a champion to me. We were all so proud of you when you won the karate tournament."

"Mom, why did you call me? I'm at work and kind of busy."

"Do you want to have lunch with me today? I'd love to see you."

"Not today. We'll do lunch tomorrow like we planned. I'm really busy, and I've got a big sales meeting I have to run to now." I felt bad having to turn her down, but she knew we were having lunch tomorrow.

"That's right, tomorrow is August 24th, and my baby is turning twenty five. I'm so excited. Your father would be so proud of you, I wish he was..." she stopped talking mid-sentence.

"I know Mom, me too. I love you. Let's talk tomorrow," I said.

"OK Champ, I love you, too," she said.

"Bye." I clicked off the phone.

I had been meaning to see her for the past couple of weeks, but things kept getting in the way. I could tell from the tone of her voice that she was feeling sad. Dad's one-year anniversary of his passing was today; he died last year. It was a shock to all of us, but especially to Mom. It all happened so fast when he got sick. I know the couple of weeks before Dad died were especially hard on Mom. They had been married for close to thirty years.

I looked at the clock on my computer; I needed to get to the meeting. I really didn't want to go but I had to. The conference room for the meeting was just down the hall. I stopped by the break area to grab a cup of coffee along the way; a few more minutes wouldn't kill me. I spent five minutes looking for the sugar. You would think a big company like this would have back-up sugar packets somewhere in the cabinets. How cheap can you get?

I decided to stop by the sales support team before going to the meeting. Antonio was there; he smiled at me as I walked over to his cube. I smiled back at him. I hated the "no dating" policy our company had, because Antonio was very cute.

My manager was strict about this as well. His comments to all of us were "don't dip your pen in the company ink," and "no fishing on the company pier." I couldn't believe someone would tell us that in this day and age. I mean really, this was my first job out of college, and as a young woman I would naturally want to date some of my co-workers. How silly can you get?

"Michelle What are you doing? Why aren't you in the big meeting?" Antonio said.

"I know, I know. I'm on my way. Hey, did you send out that proposal I turned in late yesterday?" I said.

"No, you know I didn't. I'll have it done by the end of the day. Hurry up and get to the meeting. Vic is here from Corporate," he said.

"On my way," I said.

Not Vic, I thought. He was the worst of the bunch, and he didn't like me. I wasn't one of *his* people; Vic came on board a few months after I was hired. He never got on me last year since I had a solid year. I was the number three sales rep in the entire company, but this year I was way below my numbers, and he had called me out a few times already in meetings. For some reason my sales were much lower this year, and it was really frustrating. We were deep into the third quarter for our fiscal year, and it would take a miracle if I even got close to where I was last year with my sales results.

I was feeling great at the beginning of the fiscal year; we had just gotten back from our sales trip to California. I guess I thought this year would be a breeze since I did so well last year. Unfortunately, it has not turned out that way so far. I had zero leads in my pipeline for the first quarter, since I had cleaned and scrubbed every opportunity I had at the end of the fourth quarter from last year.

Last year was a great year for me being one of the top reps. It sure felt good coming in number three out of over one hundred sales reps last year. I got a sweet year-end bonus check, and I W2'ed just over $150,000. I was expecting to bank over $200k for this year based on last year's performance, but it was not happening now. At this rate, I'd be lucky to even hit $70,000.

The big problem was that they restructured my sales territory. Last year I had four states and Washington D.C., but now they had cut me back to just Maryland, Virginia and DC. North Carolina was huge for me last year, and I had really built up a lot of pipeline deals in South Carolina for this year. I really missed having the Carolinas in my territory: it was disappointing.

The other big problem was the company jacked up my quota to almost twice what I had last year. It was a very daunting sales quota, and a large percentage of it was back-ended to the third and fourth quarters, so being behind plan now only made it that much harder for me to hit quota for the year.

But the kicker was the fact that we lost a third of the products we were selling last year. Our company merged with another company, and the geniuses at corporate decided it was best to keep the sales forces from both companies to help drive sales. So our product line was split in half with our sales region having to give up a sizable portion of our products. Plus we lost a lot of our popular products which I knew inside and out. I really hated all the changes. I wish I had the same playing field I had last year with my territory and product line. Then I would be fine with the huge increase in my quota. As it stood now I really had no chance to make quota for the year. I really hated being stuck at the bottom of the sales rankings when I was a top performer last year.

My phone vibrated, and I glanced down. It was a text from *"Josh Boyfriend."* We had a date planned for tonight to get a head start celebrating my birthday tomorrow. *"Hey baby, still a GO tonight? Love u."*

I texted back, *"Yes. C U at 7."*

Text came right back, *"Great. Pick you up at your place."*

I hope he's in a good mood tonight and doesn't badger me about the "kid issue" again. It seems like every time we've gotten together lately he's been dropping hints about kids or indirectly giving me ultimatums. I'm so tired of having the same conversation. I am not ready to settle down yet and he knows it. Just because the clock is ticking for him doesn't mean I have to do what he wants. I love him, but sometimes I feel like I need a break from this relationship. Why is he picking me up tonight? I thought we were going to meet at the restaurant.

Two

I made it to the conference room, opened the door, and tried to sneak in without being seen. Vic, our beloved VP of Sales, was on the lookout for me. He saw me right away as he stopped talking, and immediately walked directly towards me. He took a few seconds while he looked me up and down; his eyes gleamed a little bit while he checked me out. He was such a lech.

"What in the world is going on? Miss Parker, why weren't you here on time for this meeting?" Vic said.

Oh great, I was going to be the target for this meeting. Vic was dressed in a light blue double-breasted suit with a flowery pink tie on. He flicked his left wrist a bit to show off the thick gold Rolex watch with blue face that he was so proud of, then he shook his right arm down the side of his body and I saw a flash of the thick bright gold bracelet around his right wrist. Vic was not that tall; in fact, he was kind of short. I was just less than five foot nine, and Vic was about six inches shorter than me. He had a full head of semi-curly, dark black hair - not bad for an old guy. Vic swelled his chest as he stood in front of me waiting for me to respond to his attack.

He looked up at me with his dark brown eyes; they were pulsating as he stared at me.

I thought it best to remain silent and just take whatever was coming to me. I tried to find a seat in the back but they were all taken, so I took one of the spots up front. I sat down as quickly as I could so I could blend in with the others. There were about thirty people crammed into the conference room. I saw one of the speaker-phones on the table, so it was a good bet more people were listening in at corporate. Vic thrived on being the big shot.

"Can you please tell us all why you were not able to get to this meeting on time? No one else was late to the meeting. Huh, Miss Parker? What were you doing that was so important?" Vic said. I didn't respond to his question. I tried to keep my silent strategy going.

"We're waiting! I am so tired of this shit. I am not continuing with this meeting until you explain yourself, Miss Parker!" I am not sure why he kept calling me by my last name.

"I was talking to a customer. I tried my best to end the call on time, but it ran a few minutes past the start of the meeting," I replied.

"I see. Well that is good. I always like it when our sales reps are on the phone talking business. How big was the order?" Vic said.

"Sir?" I said, not understanding what he meant.

"Don't give me that 'sir' shit! How big was the fucking order you got from the customer call you were on? Miss Parker, we are in the sales business. Fuck! I want to know the dollar amount of that order," Vic said.

"Uh…" I hesitated a moment, not knowing what I was going to say. "I didn't get the order; it was just a follow-up call. I was checking in to see how their evaluation of our software was going."

I knew what was coming next. I wish I had not come to work today.

"Evaluation? Evaluation! Motherfucker! Are you kidding me? I can't fucking believe this! You know our company policy this year is no more evaluations of our software. Parker, you know this!" Vic's body was shaking as he yelled at me, and I could see the curls on his head bounce up and down every time he said the "F" word.

"I know, I'm aware of the company policy on evaluations. This is one of the last ones left over from last year. They have until the end of this month on the eval," I said.

This seemed to get Vic going even more. "What the fuck are you telling me? Are you saying this customer *(Vic used the air quotes motion with his fingers when he said customer)* has been using our fucking software for free for more than, what, nine months? Fuck! This is fucking unbelievable! Colin, what kind of ship are you running here? I want this fucking evaluation shut down today. Not tomorrow - today! Colin, do you understand what I'm saying?"

Colin was my manager. He turned to Vic and replied, "Yes sir, I will get it done right away. Michelle has a bad habit of getting around the company policies. I thought I had caught all of her free evaluations but somehow I missed this one."

"Son of a bitch! I don't want any more free evaluations out there. Parker, how many more of these free evaluations do you have?" Vic said.

I hung my head. "Two more."

"What the fuck is this! Parker, get together with Colin and get them fucking revoked. I don't want any more free evaluations out there. And if anybody else has any out there, get them addressed ASAP, and I fucking mean it," Vic said.

"Sir, I don't have any free evaluations. I abide by all of the company rules," Todd chimed in.

"Thank you, Mr. Jamison, that is good to know," Vic said. Todd was such a suck up; he got hammered in the last meeting, so now he was trying to make amends.

"Alright, let's get back to the business we were discussing before we were so rudely interrupted by Miss Parker," Vic said.

I knew this was coming. Eventually someone was going to find out about the evaluations I had out there. I just wish it hadn't come out this way. This was not good at all. I settled into my seat, opened up my notebook, and picked up my pen so that I'd be ready to take notes from the imperial Vic.

"Well, ok now. Now that we're finished with that fucking situation I can continue with what I was saying. Colin, put that slide up now." Vic motioned to Colin.

I knew what was coming next; Colin hit a few keystrokes on his laptop, then the slide was projected on the screen for all of us to see. It was our current sales ranking list for the year in our region: thirty-one sales reps listed from top sales to the lowest sales. I was number twenty-eight on the list: how demoralizing. Vic really knew how to pump us up.

"I want all of you to take a close look at the rankings. Good job to those of you above your quota, and by my count that is only nine of you. At the end of the day the company expects all of you to be above quota. That's what a fucking quota is - the bare minimum expected of you to keep your jobs! Come on people, what is the problem? I want you all to reach out to your customers every day. There is a lot of low hanging fruit out there for the taking," Vic said.

I tried to disappear as best I could. God, I would give anything to be anywhere else than in this meeting. Vic walked directly in front of me and looked me straight in the eye. His gold watch flashed on his left wrist as he shook it to make it stand out for all of us to see. I can't remember how many times Vic had told us the story of how he earned the Rolex watch at his previous company by winning a yearly sales contest five years in a row.

"Miss Parker, what is wrong with you this year? Can you tell me where your name is on the rankings?" Vic said.

Why me? I hate this job. "Um, number twenty eight," I said.

"Speak up, Miss Parker! I want everyone to hear this," Vic said.

"Number twenty eight," I said with more conviction.

"You say it as if you are proud of your performance. This is not acceptable, Miss Parker. You were one of the top sales reps last year. What is your problem?" Vic said.

I was silent, hoping it was a rhetorical question.

"I want to know. Please enlighten us, Miss Parker. I want to hear what you have to say!"

"Well, I've got a good pipeline built. I'm just waiting for some of those deals to close. I've also had a hard time adjusting to the new product realignment," I said.

"Excuses, fucking excuses, Miss Parker. Do you remember what Vince Lombardi said? 'Excuses make cowards of us all.' I think the problem is with *you*, Miss Parker," Vic said.

Oh no, not the Vince Lombardi quote again. I looked it up once after Vic kept saying it to us, and I could not find anywhere where Vince Lombardi said that.

"To be successful in sales, it's either in your DNA or not. Salespeople are born, not made. I firmly believe this. Miss Parker, maybe you have to accept the fact that it's not in your DNA. Your father was an average salesman at best; I think you are just like your father," Vic said.

Now that was uncalled for. I know Vic had some kind of history with my dad years ago. My father had pulled a few strings to help me get into this company. He thought it would be a good starting point in my career and I would learn a lot about the corporate world. Was this Vic's cheap payback? I wish I had the guts to say something to Vic, but I was resigned to just take it. I looked down at the table as I hung my head.

"At the end of the day, the company expects more from you, Miss Parker." Vic walked back to the front of the room away from me. I looked up to see what was coming next.

"This is why I am here. We have to get our fucking numbers up. Our company is currently at 63% of plan for the year. This is not acceptable. Failure is not a fucking option on my team! I expect more from all of you. I have a lot on my plate, so I can't keep watching you like a hawk. We need all hands on deck so we can all make our quotas for the year. It's a win-win for all of us. You were all hired for a fucking reason, now show us why you are all champions," Vic said.

"I want you all to look closely at this," Vic motioned to the screen. "I am here to tell you today that any sales rep below quota at the end of the year will be fucking fired. Yes, fired! I want you all to live and breathe this thought. You want to keep your jobs, its fucking simple: make quota! Colin, put up the second slide."

"Yes, now we're talking," Colin said. A few 'yeses' went around the room. The slide was a picture of a hot young woman in a bikini walking hand-in-hand with a handsome guy in a bathing suit. They were on a beach with pristine blue water behind them.

"Our 100% trip this year is going to be in West Palm Beach, FL, at the Ritz Carlton. The company is sparing no expense for those of you who earn this privilege.

And at the end of the fucking day, I expect all of you to be there. If not, then you will be looking for another job!" Vic said.

"Is that girl going to come with us?" Todd asked.

"Great question, Mr. Jamison. I will talk to our travel department to see if they can arrange it," Vic said.

A few whoops and hollers went up from the men in the room. Hillary, one of the women sales reps, looked at me and rolled her eyes.

"OK, that's it. Now get back to work. Close, close, close. I want you all to focus on closing deals! Keep the fucking business coming in so you can drink a beer with me in Florida."

Three

"That was unprofessional. You should talk to HR," Hillary said. I was back in my cube at my desk. Hillary had stopped by after the meeting.

"No, HR won't do anything. Vic has way too much power. Everyone does what he says," I replied.

"You're right, but it stinks. I hated having to listen to Vic go on and on in the meeting. It's the same old thing every time. Get your numbers up or you're fired. It's so monotonous. And what's up with the language? Seems like every other word from him is the 'F' word," Hillary said.

"I know. But it's our lot in life now. Nothing you or I can do about it," I said.

"You always have options. Especially you: you're young, single, and have no kids. You don't have to put up with this BS. Look at me: I'm married with two kids, and my husband is in between jobs. I am locked in here; I need the paycheck, but more importantly I need the health-care for my family. I feel like such a hostage." Hillary sounded so defeated.

"I know what you mean, but I want to stick it out. My dad helped me get this job, so out of respect to him, I will do my best," I said.

"Vic should have never brought up your father like that in the meeting," Hillary said. "I hate this company."

"Let's get back to work." I saw Colin walking towards us.

"Right, talk later," Hillary said as she turned to walk back to her cube at the other end of the room.

"Michelle, let's meet in my office. It's time for our one-on-one," Colin said.

"OK, I'll be right there."

* * *

"Why did Vic have to embarrass me like that in front of everyone in the meeting today?" I asked.

"I can't speak for Vic. You know his style. It should be no surprise to you," Colin said.

"I know, but it's so unprofessional. And why does he have to cuss so much?" I said.

"I don't know why he cusses so much. Maybe that's how they talk at corporate in New York. Now let's look at your weekly activity report. I have a few questions about some of your calls this week; you didn't put a code in the file log." Colin was doing his best to change the subject.

"You know what? I don't want to go through that now. I'll update all of your codes by the end of the day today. I want you to talk to HR about Vic's unprofessionalism," I responded.

"I'm sorry Michelle, but it's not my place to do that."

"Aren't you my manager? You should stick up for me, right?"

"That's not how it works. You are welcome to contact Human Resources yourself. We do have a standard email process for submitting complaints. I suggest you do that," Colin said.

"Alright, let's finish this meeting so I can go back and make my calls." I angrily stormed out of his office after we were done.

* * *

Finally, the day was over. I can't believe I used to like this job. Every day now was worse than the day before.

I stopped by Hillary's cube as I was leaving. "Have a good weekend."

"You got big plans for your birthday?" Hillary said.

"Josh and I are going out to dinner tonight. It's a surprise where we're going. Tomorrow? Not much. I'll have brunch with my mom," I said.

"Well, if you want to do something tomorrow night let me know. I'll see if I can get out of the house and we can do a girls night," Hillary said.

"See you later. Thanks Hillary."

I made it to my car and looked forward to the weekend but was not eager to return to work on Monday. The sense of frustration just kept growing day by day with this job.

* * *

Josh and I sat down in the bar area of the restaurant. It was one of those "guy" steakhouses downtown. I think it was the place Josh always went to when he was out with his buddies. I didn't complain; I was happy to be out of work and in a normal environment talking to regular people.

The waiter stopped by our table. Josh said, "I'll have a beer: your special on tap," and then Josh looked at me.

"I'll just have a glass of water for now." The waiter nodded his head as he backed away from the table. It was pretty crowded. Everyone was talking loud, and letting loose on a Friday night.

"You look very pretty tonight. How was your day at work?" Josh asked.

"I don't want to talk about my day. How about you?" I replied. Josh was a lawyer, six years in at a large firm downtown.

"The usual: gotta keep racking up the hours. Nothing new today. A lot of phone calls and paperwork," Josh answered.

The waiter came back with Josh's beer and my water. "Would you like an appetizer while you wait for your table?" he asked.

Josh shook his head no while waving the waiter away. He took a sip of his beer. "Ah, nice. I needed that." Josh was acting weird tonight. He seemed kind of tense.

"Michelle, I've been struggling with something for a while now. We need to talk," Josh began.

Uh oh, I've had guys break up with me before. I knew what was coming, but *now*? It was my birthday tomorrow. Really Josh! I wanted to punch him in the face. I crossed my arms while staring down at the table.

"I know what you're going to say," I responded.

Josh had a surprised look on his face. He took another sip of his beer. "Michelle, I love you, I always have, but I don't believe you love me the same way I love you." I looked up from the table glaring at him. He was sincere. I didn't say anything.

"I want to marry you, I've made it pretty clear this past year. I want to settle down with you, have kids, and start our own family. But every time I bring up the subject you ignore it. I think it's time we stopped playing this charade. I don't have the time to keep waiting for you."

OK, now it was out. His clock was ticking. He had said this many times before. Josh was thirty-two, I was twenty-four. I had told him many times that I didn't want to have kids yet, but he was relentless. Now, it had finally come to this.

"I'm sorry if you think I have led you along, but I have always been straight with you. I am not ready to have kids; my plan was to wait until I was at least thirty before starting a family. I can understand if you don't want to wait. It's probably best for us if we have some time apart," I said.

"I'm sorry to do this now since it's your birthday tomorrow, but I just can't keep doing this," he replied.

I drank some of my water, and looked around the room; lots of couples were together at the tables and the bar. They were laughing, talking, drinking: life seemed so easy for them. Why not me? I started to get angry.

"I want to go home. I'm going to call a cab."

"Michelle, come on, don't be that way. Let's have dinner. We can be friends at least."

Please! Men and women can't be friends. I got up from the table. "Bye Josh."

"Michelle, wait!"

I pulled out my cell phone to call a cab. Home is what I needed.

What an end to my week. Josh got up from the table to try and follow me, but I was already wading my way through the noisy crowd and out the front door before he could catch me. Without realizing it, I was crying: tears were streaming down my face. I was outside the restaurant and started walking east. I'd get a cab on Broadway.

Four

I woke up and looked at the clock on the nightstand; it blinked in green - 1:12. Too bad, I thought it was closer to morning. Then the thoughts came. I couldn't control them. I desperately wanted to sleep but I couldn't. Once I woke up during the night it was impossible to get back to sleep. My thoughts consumed me. I tried to be positive, but I always ended up in a bad spiral. Nothing good was happening in my life.

Thoughts about my career took over again - I hate my job, I am such a failure. Where am I going? What am I going to do with my life? I don't like doing this kind of work. Who chooses sales as a career? It's so depressing having to deal with people like Vic, and Colin doesn't care about me at all; he's a terrible boss who's just out to protect his own job. It's so futile! After today, I don't want to go back there again. Vic's treatment was so dehumanizing. I should have fought back in the meeting. Why did I just sit there and take it? Why did I do that? Am I weak?

What kind of person am I turning into? I don't really like who I am anymore. It is so frustrating dealing with these kinds of people. What is the point of life? I thought my life was going to turn out differently. I went to a good college, got excellent grades, and this is what I have to deal with: idiots who treat me like garbage. I hate this. I can't quit, though. I'm not a quitter. I need this job. I've got a lot of bills to pay, but I'm lucky that I only have a few student loans to pay off. Mom and Dad were good about helping me pay for college tuition. Right now, my monthly bills are my mortgage for the condo, car payment, student loans, and I still need to save up for retirement. I didn't want to end up as a homeless person living on the mall with a bunch of other losers. If I don't get married or have kids, then I'll have no one to take care of me.

I need something really positive to look forward to, so it's really important that I have a good paying job. But I hate where I work! Can't I get a better job? But I hate looking for a job; it's so demeaning dealing with all of the recruiters.

I just realized that it was my birthday; it's August 24th. A new day had already begun, a new year for me. Now I was twenty-five years old. I couldn't believe it. My life is in the toilet and now I'm a year older. I don't have anything good happening in my life. I need something positive. A lot of my friends from high school and college have good jobs, are in good relationships, and so many of them are very successful.

They all seem to be very happy with their lives; it all looks so easy for them.

What is their secret? Why can't I have a life like that? What is wrong with me? Why am I not having any success? I hate my job, my boyfriend dumped me, and my dad died last year. I have my mom, but she's been very depressed lately with Dad's passing. I wish I had not been an only child. It would be great to have a brother or sister now to talk to; I wouldn't be so alone. I remember when I was very young how I used to beg my parents to have another baby. Why didn't they have another kid? I was so lonely growing up.

What was the point of getting a college degree? I went to an excellent school, and I graduated with a very high GPA. Maybe I'm not cut out for corporate sales. But why would Dad want me to follow this career path? It makes no sense to me. Maybe I should get a law degree. It's not too late for that. Josh always told me I'd be an awesome lawyer since I'm so smart and have a great memory for details. My grades are definitely good enough to get into any of the top law schools. I just need to study for the LSAT; I bet I could nail it. I always did well on standardized tests.

I just don't like where I am with my life now. In five years I'll be thirty. Where will I be then? Will I still be stuck in this lousy job? Will I be married by then? Maybe I should get back together with Josh. I'm sure he would take me back; I'd just have to agree to have kids now. He is so ready to start a family. I want to have kids, but I was thinking it would be best to have kids after I'm thirty when my career will be more secure. I don't want to be a stay-at-home mom. I don't want to be dependent on my husband and his income. I want independence and freedom. I like that Mom had her own career as a lawyer. Maybe I should be a lawyer like her. Dad always felt like it was too much work: sixty to eighty hour weeks in the beginning. But Mom seemed to be happy when I was growing up. She stopped practicing the past couple years with Dad's illness and his passing. Maybe it's time for her to get back to work. I'll talk to her about it tomorrow when we get together for my birthday.

What about going into medicine? No, it takes way too long. I don't want to go to school for another ten years. I don't know what I should do. That's the problem. How do people choose the right career?

I need to think of something different. This is a bad train of thought; I need to change it. I just don't enjoy my life anymore. Work is a big part of me, but I wish I had a job that I liked, and found interesting and challenging. I don't think I can do this for the next thirty-some years. Was this the best I could do after graduating from college? I know Dad wanted me to work at this company, but I don't think this is the right place for me. Am I really cut out for this type of work as a career? I seriously doubt it. But what do I do now?

I have no other choice at this time. I have to go back to work on Monday.

Now I have no boyfriend, and no prospects for getting married. One day I'd like to have kids, but not yet. I don't want to have kids while I'm working in this dead-end job. By thirty I want to be married, but not yet. I thought Josh might have been the one; why did he have to break it off now? Did he think I was too tall for him? He always made snide comments about my height compared to his: he's five foot ten and I'm five foot nine. Whenever I wore high heels he was always a little nervous standing next to me.

I wish I hadn't been so tall. It would have been nice to be right around five foot five and weigh one hundred pounds: nice and petite. As it is I'm a giant woman. Plus my feet are so big: I'm like one of those clowns in the circus with the huge floppy shoes. Lately I've been packing on some pounds; I need to go on a diet again. I've got to get on a workout routine like when I was in school. I need to hit the gym hard and soon. Maybe I should get back into karate. I could teach some classes at my old dojo. I know my sensei would love that. She has always been after me to get back into karate and said I would be a great teacher. I should do that. What's the point of having a black belt and not using it? I enjoyed the tournaments; I was good.

I understand why Josh did what he did. He can't wait five more years to start a family; he would be thirty-seven by then. That's too long for him. I should not have gotten serious with him after we started dating, but he was so cute and nice. I have no one else to go out with now. I've been working so much lately. I have no friends. Is this my life? I don't like it. I have nothing good happening in my life: no boyfriend, no potential boyfriends. Maybe I should ask Antonio out; the hell with the company policy of employees not being able to date each other. He's cute and I know he would jump at the chance to go out with me. Maybe he has some cute friends he could introduce me to. That's a good idea. But I have no one to go out for a nice dinner with now.

I can't break this vicious cycle of thoughts. I hate waking up in the middle of the night. I can never get back to sleep. I just end up thinking. My thoughts end up controlling me: I can't stop them. I want to sleep, but I can't turn off my mind. How do other people deal with this? Is there something wrong with me?

I miss Dad. I wish he were still here. He was always there for me when I needed a pep talk; he was so positive. He loved me so much. Why did he have to leave us so early? I kept tossing and turning in bed. Sleep would not come. Too many thoughts rushing in: I tried to stop them. I kept thinking the same things over and over. Am I going mad? Is this what happens to people when they go crazy? Do I need to see a doctor? I spoke out loud, "Dad, I wish you were here. I miss you so much!" The tears came again, but this time they were tears of despair.

When I cried at the restaurant, it wasn't because Josh was breaking up with me. It's my life: I can't do anything right. I'm a failure. I hate my job. Josh and I had been going sideways for months now. It was no surprise, but I just feel so bad about myself and where my life is headed.

I tried to think of something positive that would make me happy. I needed to change how I felt. I have to control my thoughts. I need something encouraging to think about. Do I have *anything* good in my life? Think!

I remembered the last vacation I took with Dad. We were in Cancun: one of our favorite spots. The Caribbean was a perfect blue: so beautiful. The baby waves were slowly rolling up to the sandy beach, gently lapping against the white sand. I remember we played tennis more than we swam in the ocean. When was that? I tried to remember. It must have been my sophomore or junior year of college. I remember how hard we played tennis, with neither one of us giving in to the other.

This was not working. I was feeling worse now. I looked over at my nightstand. My bottle of sleeping pills was there. I picked up the bottle; it was unopened and felt heavy in my hand. How many pills would it take? I had no idea, but if I took all of them, I bet that would be enough. At least I would not have to deal with all of these negative thoughts controlling me. I am losing myself. Where am I? I sat up in my bed. I can't stay here anymore. I might completely lose it.

No, I will not make that choice now. I shook my head from side to side to physically accept my decision then threw the bottle of sleeping pills against the wall, and it bounced under the bed. I had to get out of the house. I put on a pair of sweatpants and a t-shirt. I knew exactly where I needed to go.

I got into my car in the garage and turned the ignition on to start the car. I forgot to open the garage door. Or was that on purpose? The car was running. How long would it take? I rolled down all of the car windows. The smell of the exhaust quickly started to filter into the car. No, I can't do that. I pushed the button on the garage door opener, and the door engaged and rolled up. The cool air from outside immediately flowed into the car. Even though my life stinks right now, it will get better. It has to.

Five

I drove down the road with the car windows open; the fresh air on my face felt soothing. I was almost there. I turned onto the little side road. It was just past two thirty in the morning, but the church was always open. Dad used to bring us here all the time. He would bring us late at night when we needed to say a prayer if something was going on in our lives or our extended family's lives. My dad didn't like going to the formal services; he really didn't follow any one religion. He always joked that this was his personal church when we came at night because very often no one else was there. It was our family sanctuary.

I pulled open the heavy exterior door of the church with my left hand. In my right hand I carried a small bouquet of flowers. It was quiet inside away from the road: very peaceful. I took a deep breath through my nose while I closed my eyes for a moment. Yes, this was better. My head started to clear a little bit. The water fountain with the holy water was bubbling. I put my left hand in the water then touched my forehead.

I walked to the church's interior entrance and looked inside: no one was there. I loved this church because it reminded me of Dad. I remember the time he brought me here when Mom was sick. It was not serious; she had bronchitis. I was thirteen or fourteen, I can't remember exactly. We prayed here together for close to an hour for Mom. I was really scared that she might die, but Dad reassured me she would be fine. He had that way about him where he always made me feel secure. I loved coming to the church with Dad; it was our special time together as father and daughter.

The church was dimly lit. I felt a mixture of happiness and sadness upon entering. As I walked to the front of the church, I could clearly see the stained glass windows with their paintings reflected by the low light. Two candle stations flanked the altar. Each one held close to thirty candles, many of which were already lit. I walked to the right side where there were a few unlit candles, picked up a match, and lit a candle for my father. I sat in one of the pews and knelt down on my knees.

I closed my eyes while I put my hands together and rested them against my forehead in prayer. "Dear Father, please help me." I sat there for a long time trying not to think of anything. I don't know how long I was there with my eyes closed. I tried to clear my mind as best I could. Slowly I got up from my knees to sit on the pew and began to open my eyes. The silence was comforting as I sat there. I understood now why my dad liked coming to the church late at night. It felt like the church was mine: just there for me. I smiled remembering how my dad used to say this was his private church, and when I was a little kid I believed him. I crossed myself and said, "Amen." I grabbed my flowers and slowly walked out of the church, pushing the heavy outside door with the right side of my body.

The air was crisp outside for a late summer night. Fall was just around the corner. I looked up at the bright and vibrant stars in the clear night sky. I walked away from the church towards the graveyard. There was some light in the sky from a half moon. I made my way meandering through the headstones to the back of the graveyard. I had been here many times before and knew exactly where I was going.

I put the flowers down on the ground in front of the headstone. *Daddy, I love you.* I sat cross-legged on the dry grass; the sprinklers usually came on at dawn. I focused on breathing in through my nose and out through my mouth, just as my karate training had taught me.

My anxieties from earlier in the night drained away. My breathing was slow and easy. I felt so much better sitting next to my dad even though he was gone. I still felt his presence at times like this sitting on the grass next to him. Dad was my champion; he loved me so much and was always there to cheer me on. I didn't realize it at the time when I was growing up, but he was always there for me when I needed him. I was lucky to have a dad like him. I just wished he were still here with me. The pain sometimes was just too much to bear. Why did he have to die? It was so unfair.

I had never had someone close to me die before. I didn't fully understand the finality of death until after Dad was gone. When a person dies, that's it. It's over. You will never see that person again in your life. It has taken me some time to adjust to Dad being gone.

Sometimes I catch myself thinking that I'll see Dad next weekend at his house or we'll play tennis next week. I don't know how many times I have picked up my phone to call Dad at home only to realize he was not there anymore. The reality of death is painful. It would have been great to have Dad meet my future husband and children; he would have been an awesome grandfather.

I just wish I could see him one more time, talk to him, be with him, hear him laugh, and see him smile. Death is so unforgiving, and especially when someone you love dies, it stays with you forever. I am always going miss Dad. Every day of my life I know I will think of him.

"Dad, do you remember the time when I won the ka-rate tournament when I was sixteen? You were the only person who really thought I could win. I could not have done it without you. I wish you were…" I stopped talking. It was too painful.

I sat there, closed my eyes, and tried to control my thoughts and not think of anything. The silence was reassuring.

Images went by in my head—

I saw my dad teaching me how to ride a bike. He put me on top of my green bike and pushed it forward to get me going. He said, "You can do it Meeshy!" I started pedaling. I was doing it, but I couldn't steer. I pedaled my bike about thirty feet then I crashed into a parked car on the street—

Hiking with Dad and Mom in the mountains, me complaining about not wanting to go any further, and Dad encouraging me, "Come on Michelle, we're almost at the top. You can do it!" I remember Dad being so happy once we reached the top of the ridge, looked out over the plains, and the three of us enjoyed some water and granola bars—

I lost the karate championship match. I was fourteen years old, sitting on the bleacher seats, crying and crying. I was heartbroken, but Dad was there rubbing my shoulder, "Sweetheart, I am so proud of you. You did your best, and that's all you can ask. You can win it next year." He sat by my side as I cried—

Dad and I are walking on a beach with the waves lapping at our feet. He is chasing me, I am giggling, and he is laughing. I must have been six or seven years old—

I'm at my college graduation walking around outside looking for Mom and Dad. I see Dad first: he was staring right at me with the biggest smile on his face. Tears were running down his cheeks; he was so proud. He couldn't contain his enthusiasm. He runs to me, "Michelle!" he yells and grabs me in a bear hug. He whispers in my ear, "Way to go Meeshy. Way to go!"—

I'm at the hospital at Dad's bedside. Mom is on the other side of the bed. Dad is sleeping. He looks so peaceful and free of pain while he's sleeping. This is my last image of him before he dies.

Six

I returned home and was now fast asleep in my bed. Usually I don't dream much, but now I was having a series of very vivid dreams.

I was all alone in a conference room at work, just sitting there, waiting at the conference table. The door opened and a young woman in a sharp looking, black, professional dress came in. She had blonde hair tied up in a bun and was wearing black horn-rimmed glasses. She didn't smile; her lips, covered in a dark red lipstick, were pursed together tightly, which gave her face a solemn look. Her eyes were a dull blue: not much life in them.

"Hello, my name is Jamie Matthews. I am with Blue Sky Consulting. Thank you for coming to this meeting."

I didn't know what to say. I was there already. I smiled at her but she didn't smile back. She just stared at me. No, not really at me: it was more like she was looking at the wall behind me, over my left shoulder.

"Here is your packet." Jamie leaned over to push a blue-green folder at me.

I looked at the packet. On the cover was a picture montage: one photo is a young woman hiking in the mountains, another displays a young man windsurfing on a lake, one features a middle aged man sitting in front of a fountain in what looked to be Florence, Italy, and the last is a middle aged woman sitting on a beach chair in Hawaii. All nice pictures, I thought, but what did they have to do with me?

"Open the packet, there's a letter in there for you," Jamie said.

I opened it to look inside. "Dear Michelle..... We regret to inform you............" Now it made sense, I was being laid off. They hired an outside consultant to come in and do the dirty work. My company was a bunch of losers. No one had the guts to tell me face-to-face that I was being let go.

Jamie handed me an envelope as she explained, "Here is your severance check. I now need your employee identification badge along with your key card. As we speak, your personal office belongings are being boxed up for your retrieval. All your logins and passwords have been disabled. A security guard will be here any moment to escort you out of the building." She kept staring at the wall behind me and spoke in a soft monotone voice devoid of emotion.

I asked her, "Do you like your job? Doesn't it stink to give people bad news every day?"

She shifted her gaze towards my eyes for the first time as she pondered my question. She stayed silent ten seconds before responding, "Yes, I love my job. It allows me to have no feelings towards anyone or anything. I find it a lot easier to live my life this way." Her mouth opened wider as her face broke into a big smile exposing large bright white teeth.

"Ah, Ted is here to escort you out of the building."

A big beefy man stood at the conference door; I hadn't even heard him open the door. He had huge arms, a large shaved head, and was a bit taller than me. Another security guard came up behind him. He walked into the conference room carrying a box, which I assumed contained the personal belongings from my desk. The second guard placed the box on the table in front of me. "All of your personal items are in this box," he said, and then walked out of the conference room. The large security guard at the door nodded at the second guard as he left the room.

I got up to leave without saying anything to Jamie the consultant. What was there to say? I looked into my box of stuff and saw my portable clock radio, my blue glass paperweight, my small Washington Monument, and my two little toy cars. I placed the packet with the cheesy picture montage and my severance check into the box.

"Hurry up little lady, it's time to vamoose. I don't have all day," said the beefy security guard.

I don't know what happened but I finally snapped. I had had enough. This company was the worst. I was sick and tired of being treated this way. From Vic, to Colin, to this consultant, and now this rude, fat security guard!

I walked directly in front of the security guard, opened and closed my hands into fists to get the blood flowing into my arms. I tightened my legs the best that I could to warm them up. I stood face to face with him; he was taller than me by a few inches but I was confident I could take him. He looked like he hadn't done any serious exercise in a few months.

"I am going to break your nose, and there is not one thing you can do to stop me," I said.

"I like your spunk, little..." but before he could finish his sentence I put a left jab, right cross combo on him. I jabbed him hard with my left hand across his jaw, then used all the force I could muster from my legs, driving my right elbow up squarely into his nose. I felt the fleshy part of his nose give way as my elbow broke the bone.

The guard could not believe what had happened: that I would actually punch him. I am not that muscular, but

I have strong legs, and that's where you get most of your power for a solid punch. I was pumped up and ready to take on the world! It felt great. I really popped him with my elbow. The move I had done reminded me of my days in karate competition, although I had never broken anyone's nose before. I thoroughly enjoyed the sweet-spot feeling of my elbow smashing into his nose. The guard immediately put his hands up to his face to try and stop the blood from gushing out of his nose. He whined, "You broke my nose," as he scurried away to the men's bathroom.

I looked at Jamie the consultant: she was wide-eyed. "You just sit there and be quiet," I said. "You don't want to mess with me right now. I've had enough of your crap." I picked up my box of stuff and walked defiantly out of the conference room.

My dream changed. This was one of my standard dreams I've had since graduating from college. I was sitting in a huge lecture hall with my blue book in front of me. There were two ballpoint pens on the desk. The TA's were handing out the tests, but I was not ready. I had not attended this class. The professor yelled out, "You have sixty minutes starting from now. Eyes on your own paper." What do I do? I am going to fail the exam for sure; my stomach sinks with disappointment. This dream does not last long, and I can't figure out why I keep having it.

I heard a baby crying. The baby wouldn't let up, as the crying got louder and louder. In my dream, I was sleeping in a large king-sized bed. I heard myself say, "Honey, it's your turn." A man next to me in bed grunted, "OK." He got up wearily to go to the baby's room and said, "They never tell you that when you have a baby you'll never sleep again." The baby continued to cry. I tried to get out of this dream as fast as I could. I didn't want to dream about this anymore. I tried to block my mind out from this reality. The dream faded away.

Clouds are in my mind; this dream feels a lot different. It's as if I am actually living it while I'm dreaming. I'm standing on a cliff with a vast body of water before me. The water is completely still: no wind, no waves. The sun is glimmering off the water. My eyes hurt from the glare; it's so bright. I am alone. I see a ship off in the distance. It is a big ship, maybe a cruise ship. I hear people talking and laughing. I hear music and people singing. Where are they all going?

My head is warm. I fall into a deeper sleep. I jump from the cliff towards the water, but rather than fall into the water I am now flying over it. It is beautiful. I am on top of the world. I am soaring and the wind blows across my face and body as I fly. I see the vastness of the water below me. It's deep blue tinged with flecks of bright green. I wish I could be here forever. I ascend up high into the sky, and then dive directly down towards the water below. My body splashes into the water: so warm and inviting. I love the water; it's so tranquil.

I feel my eyes close. My sleep is so deep now. I no longer have thoughts. My body is numb. I try to open my eyes, but they don't respond. I try moving my arms to swim but nothing happens. My conscious mind has disappeared. I can't control my thoughts anymore. I have no thoughts. I feel my body floating down into the water: deeper, darker, and deeper into the abyss. The water has absorbed me. My mind and body have no consciousness. I try to wake up from the dream but I can't. I try to think but no thoughts come. I am nothing.

Seven

I was sitting at my kitchen table having my morning cup of coffee. Weekends are great: you can sit and take your time drinking your coffee. I was always late getting to work on weekdays, so I had to take my coffee from home or get an awful cup at the office. I enjoyed Saturday mornings because I could totally kick back, relax, and take it easy.

Last night was behind me. It was a rough night. The dark thoughts were getting stronger and stronger lately. I don't want to think about it now. I hope it doesn't keep happening.

I was on my laptop surfing, checking out the social world on the Internet. People call it "social media" but I think the more appropriate term now is "social advertising;" just way too many ads being pushed to me when I'm online.

I saw a lot of birthday wishes from people that I know well and even some who I don't really know. It made me feel good to see some of the people who messaged me: very nice. I tried not to be online too much lately since so much of the content was so depressing to me. I mean how many pictures of kids and people on vacation could I take? Kids birthdays', kids being born, kids going to school, kids riding their bikes, kids swimming, kids making faces, kids playing with cats, kids playing with dogs, and kids doing all things imaginable. I don't have kids, so relating to people with children is a real challenge. They are all so obsessed with their kids.

The vacation pictures were tough to stomach as well— people visiting beaches, lakes, mountain hikes, exotic cities around the world, bicycle trips, and here I am stuck at home having to work every day. I thought these websites were supposed to make you feel better about yourself and more connected to your friends and family, but it was having the exact opposite effect on me. The more I was on the social websites, the more depressed I became about my life. It just emphasized that I wasn't married, didn't have kids, had a terrible job, and didn't travel. The social world on the Internet was just too "look at me" based. Sometimes I think I would be happier if I'd cut myself off from all of these social sites.

Suddenly my front doorbell rang. Who could be coming to my place this early on a Saturday? I looked at the clock on my computer: 8:56. It was too early for the door-to-door people. I walked to the front door and looked through the window: it was Mom. A pang of fear went through my body; I hoped everything was all right. I quickly unlocked the door to let her in.

"Mom, what is it? Is everything OK?"

"Yes, everything's fine. Happy birthday, Champ."

"Thank you. Why are you here so early? What's going on?" I gave her a hug, kissed her on the cheek, and then closed the door as she came in. She was carrying Dad's old briefcase.

"I know we planned on lunch today, but I have a gift for you that couldn't wait," she said.

"Really? You couldn't give it to me at lunch today?" I asked.

"Let's sit down." She walked towards the kitchen.

"*Mom*, you're being so mysterious." I kind of whined like a five year old when I said "Mom."

"Can I get a cup of coffee? I see you've already made some," she said.

"Sure."

What was going on? Mom was not one for birthday surprises. I got her a cup of coffee and sat down next to her at the kitchen table as I placed the coffee in front of her.

"OK. Tell me why you're here. Why do you have Dad's briefcase?" I asked.

Mom gathered herself at the table before talking, sipped her coffee, and closed her eyes as she took a deep breath. I hoped what she had to tell me was not too serious; Mom was very anxious.

"Michelle, I am so proud of you. You are my only child and I love you. I have only loved one other person in the world as much as I love you." Mom went silent and dug out a Kleenex from her purse. I stayed quiet. This was not like Mom to share her feelings this way. She was not an expressive or outwardly affectionate person.

She continued, "As you know, this is a bittersweet birthday for you. You're turning twenty-five today, and one year ago your father passed away, just one day before your birthday. I know it's been hard on you. No child should lose their father that way. I have tried my best to comfort and reassure you, but this past year has taken a toll on me. I didn't realize how much we all depended on your dad. He was the glue that held our family together. Losing him has been…" She stopped talking, and this time she broke down in tears. Tears were coming down my cheeks, too. I couldn't control them.

"Mom, we're going to be OK. We have each other now. No one can take that away from us."

We embraced in a silent hug. I put my head on her chest and felt her heart beating loudly. She wrapped her arms around me and held me close. She smelled of lavender from her body lotion. Slowly her crying subsided. We maintained our silent embrace for a few minutes. Mom was the first to pull away.

"Michelle, I have a birthday gift for you from your father."

What did she say? I didn't understand what she meant.

"What are you talking about?" I asked.

"I know it's hard to believe, but your father planned this out a few weeks before he passed away." She picked up the briefcase, placed it on the table, and clicked it open.

She pulled out a large manila envelope; it looked quite heavy. "Here it is. I have not opened it; it's still sealed. Your father specifically told me this was only for you. He gave me strict instructions to give it to you on your twenty-fifth birthday. He was very adamant about that."

I didn't know what to say, a gift from Dad. He's been gone for a year now. I took the large envelope from Mom. It was very heavy, and I had to hold it with two hands. It felt like a large binder of paper was inside. I set it on the table in front of me and stared at it. On the outside of the yellow envelope was written "Michelle" and nothing else.

"Should I open it now?"

"No, I think it's best you open it when you're alone."

"OK, I'll get in touch with you when I'm done."

"Let me know later if you still want to do lunch or dinner tonight."

"I will. I have no idea how long this will take. I think it's a letter or some kind of document for me," I said. Mom smiled at me.

"I love you, Champ. I only wish the best for you. This has been a hard year for both of us," Mom said.

"I know. The next year has to be better for both of us. Mom, I want to talk to you later today about your career. Are you ready to go back to work?"

"Sure, we can talk about it. Actually, I have been thinking the same thing lately. One year is long enough to be in mourning."

"I'm glad you feel that way."

I saw her out the door, and she left with a big smile on her face. It was the happiest I've seen her in a long time. Mom went through so much when Dad died; he was diagnosed with pancreatic cancer the previous year. He battled it as best he could, but he only lasted seven months after the diagnosis. For most of the last eighteen months Mom's life has been so stressful, and so has mine.

I went back to the kitchen table. I picked up the large, yellow manila envelope, and held it in my hands. What could it be? I got a sharp knife out of the knife holder on the kitchen counter and cut the envelope open. I stuck my hand inside: it was a binder of paper. I pulled it out. It was kind of big; there were a lot of pages. It looked like it was bound at a local copy store. There was nothing written on the blue cover. I opened it to the first page: "For Michelle" is how it started. A rush of blood went through my body, and my head felt woozy. I put the binder down on the table. I needed to lie down. I went to the couch in the living room. I needed to catch my breath before reading it. *OK, I can do this.* I picked up the binder and a piece of paper fell to the floor. It was a single sheet: a handwritten note to me.

Dear Michelle,

I know you might find this odd hearing from me after I have passed away. I wanted to leave something behind for you: some of my thoughts based on my life experiences and now death. I have written a rather long and somewhat rambling letter to you. I started writing it a week after my cancer diagnosis. I tried to write as much as I could these past months. Some days were better than others. I didn't write this as a medical journal. That would be too boring and somewhat gloomy.

I wrote this to help you as you move forward in your life since I will not be there to help you and love you as a father should. I am heartbroken. This is the hardest part of dying - knowing I will not be there for you.

I am writing now on August 20, a few days before your 24th birthday. I know the end is near for me, so I wanted to make sure I wrote this note to help you better understand why I did this. The past few years, way before I got sick, I had been thinking about writing some kind of auto-biography to leave behind for you after I was gone. And now my cancer has forced me to write it in a somewhat abbreviated and rushed fashion. I wish I had started it sooner because I feel I have left some things out that I wanted to tell you, but now looking at this document and what I've written the past few months, I am pleased I did take the time and effort to write this for you.

Well, here it is, the letter starts in late January earlier this year. I hope you have a great 25th birthday. You are my greatest creation. I did nothing better in my life than being your father, and I regret now that I was not able to spend more time with you when you were growing up. Those special moments of your life were a treasure to me.

Love,

Dad

For Michelle

January 24 Journal Entry

This is my first entry. I have wanted to do this for a long time but just never got around to doing it, and now time is getting short for me.

It's been about five days now since I found out I have cancer. I still can't believe it. I don't think I have fully accepted it. I always thought I'd live into my eighties. I've never been really sick before. I eat well, I exercise, I don't smoke, I don't drink much, and overall I live a healthy life. It's just so unfair. I keep thinking over and over - why is this happening to me? How can I get cancer?

I'm hoping tomorrow my doctor will tell me this is all a mistake - that they mixed up the lab results or something and I am completely fine. How can I die now? I am only fifty-seven years old. I don't have any family history of pancreatic cancer. Somehow I wish this would all be worked out and that I'm completely healthy.

I just don't want to think about dying now. It's way too early for me. I have you and your Mom and my responsibilities as a father and a husband. I have always been healthy. This just makes no sense to me.

I know how hard this is for you and your mother. It's difficult for all of us as a family. You are young - you have your whole life ahead of you. I hate to see you go through all of this. I've done some research the past few days. Dying from cancer is brutal for the patient, family, and friends. The odds for me beating this are long. The cancer I have is one of the worst.

I don't intend this to be a medical journal. I want to write down my thoughts and life experiences for you. I don't have much to leave behind for you, so maybe you can benefit from my life experiences. Plus, I think writing in a journal will be therapeutic. Maybe it will help me through the difficult journey I have ahead.

The first thought I have is about how stupid I have been in my life. Your whole viewpoint on life changes when you find out that you are going to die. When you're young, you never think about dying - there's always tomorrow. My whole life I've put off stuff I wanted to do and procrastinated because I knew I could do it tomorrow. I wasted so much time in my life by not doing things because I always put them off. There were so many things I wanted to do when I was young but never got around to doing them. Most of my adulthood I have been doing things for other people due to my responsibilities—work, husband, father, my parents, my extended family, friends, our house. I can't remember the last time I just did something I wanted to do for myself. It's my own fault - I have no one to blame but myself. Seems like the thirty-two years since I started my work career have gone by without me really fully living my life. I know I'm not making sense, but I'm just writing my feelings now as I think of where I am today, finding out my tomorrows are limited. I started my work career at twenty-five, married at thirty-two, and became a dad two years later - huge life responsibilities you never relinquish. I never planned or dreamed of being an "account manager" in corporate sales. I just happened into it and never got out of it. Again, I have no one to blame but myself. I don't want this journal to be a bitch session from me but I want you to know how I feel about my life now as I look back. Twenty-five was the pivotal year for my life. You will be twenty-five next year.

January 26 Journal Entry

I don't think I'll write much today which will be of value to you. I'm still very angry. I am finding it hard to focus and think straight. I realize now that the doctor is not going to come in and tell me this is all a mistake. My new reality is true. I do have cancer. My anger and rage are hard to control. Why me? It's just not fair - I don't deserve this. I have lived a good life. I have so much more to do with my life. I need to be there for you and your mom. Just the thought of me not being there for you is killing me. I can't take it. I have no patience for anyone now. I don't want to talk to anybody. I don't want any nurses trying to make chitchat with me. Yes, I have cancer, and I am most likely going to die. I will fight it as best as I can but the percentage of survival is against me. It's not a winnable battle. The more I think about it, the angrier I get. I just keep thinking it's not fair, and this should not be happening to me.

I guess it doesn't matter how you live your life, because I lived an exemplary life and in the end it makes no difference. I'm going to die way too early. My life will be cut short. It's just not right. I deserved better.

February 9 Journal Entry

It's taken me a while to write again. The past couple of weeks my anger and disappointment have prevented me from focusing on anything specific. I'd give anything in my life to cure my cancer. I would be so thankful. But it's not going to happen. I understand that now.

I want to start writing more about my life - especially some of my mistakes that I hope you don't repeat.

What are my regrets? What could I have done differently? Looking back on my life, I see so many situations where I regret what I did or didn't do. I see so many instances of not taking action or not doing things that I wanted to do, had planned to do, or dreamed of doing when I was young. What held me back? Why didn't I live my life to its fullest? Was it fear? Was it complacency? Was it worry? Did I take the easy path because I didn't want to take any risks? Why did I lose touch with friends and family as I got older? Why wasn't I able to make new friends when I got older like I did when I was younger? Why did I just live my life on cruise control in my adulthood? I was so focused on what I *had* to do versus what I *wanted* to do.

I was really good at playing baseball when I was a kid. In little league, from nine years old until I was fifteen, I was always one of the best players on the field. I didn't stick with it when I got older and entered high school. I wish my parents had pushed me more to continue playing baseball. If I had practiced more and worked harder when I was sixteen and seventeen, there was a good chance I could have gotten a college scholarship to a decent school in Arizona or California. What happened? Why did I quit baseball? I got scared and intimidated by the other players. I was one of the bigger and faster kids from the time I was nine until I was fourteen, but then I stopped growing. I was a late grower and did not reach my full height until I was eighteen. I didn't know what was happening, and I just thought I was not good anymore and couldn't compete with the other kids who were outgrowing me. Looking back, I am very sad I quit. When you quit, it's gone forever and you never get it back. I didn't know it then, but I would learn more life lessons in the future about quitting.

Why did I keep working in the same field all my life? I was good at it, but not the best. I made decent money, but I never advanced into executive management or had the guts to start my own business. I was always just above average. I never became rich in a financial sense. I never created anything for myself. I worked for over thirty years and I have nothing to show for it - no equity. I was just a worker bee. Now, near the end, I see this as a major failure in my life.

I wish I had learned how to be more creative in general during my life. I had no musical skills. I tried to play instruments when I was young but none of them ever took and I never enjoyed it. In recent years, I saw a lot of my family and friends playing in bands on the weekends—I saw how happy they were when they played. It was a big part of their lives, and I envied them.

Besides music, there were so many other options open to me—painting, writing, photography—but nothing ever clicked for me, or maybe I just never put forth the effort necessary.

I wish I had been more creative in my life, because now I leave nothing behind. Is that important to me? Yes, for two reasons - it would have been cool to leave something tangible behind that I created, and it would have benefited my life to tap into my creative abilities. The sad part is that I never even tried to be creative with my work or hobbies. The best way to fail is to not even try. That is me - I never had the ambition, guts, or patience to tap into my creative abilities. Now I really wish I had done more of that. Rather than being a robot at work, I might have enjoyed my life more and been fully engaged in my career by better utilizing my creative abilities.

I wasted so many hours of my life watching TV shows, and sports, sitting like a zombie in front of the television. I don't regret missing any TV shows or movies in my life, but I do regret the time I wasted just zoning out in front of the TV - again, another failure. I wonder what else I could have done with my life if I had used that wasted time in a creative and productive manner.

I know I'm rambling here, but this is something important I want you to understand. Michelle, look at your life now. Take a step back from yourself and look objectively. Are you being creative? In your work? During your down time?

All of us have creative abilities. You just have to try. Once you try, you will get better, but you will never know unless you try. I could have done more with my life if I had only tried more. Don't be afraid. I remember how much I loved to read when I was young. It was a great escape. I learned a lot, and I felt a lot when I read an interesting and moving story. When I was a teenager, I dreamed of one day becoming a writer, but I never followed up on it. I didn't even try. I was too intimidated. As I got older, I thought only smart and talented people became writers. I didn't look at myself as a writer. My self-image did not match my dream. The pain of regret for never trying is a very heavy burden to bear. Yes, I'm feeling it now.

I feel you have many talents. You are very smart - much smarter than me. I remember your musical ability - you played the piano very well until you gave it up when you were thirteen. Now looking back, your mom and I should have pushed you to continue with your piano lessons. You were not a prodigy, but you had a talent for it.

It doesn't matter what you do creatively, but do something. Don't avoid being creative in your life because you never tried. Lose yourself in the creative process. It is a gift that we all have, but you have to tap into it, nourish it, build on it, and over time it will get stronger.

February 10 Journal Entry

Today I went through my personal library - I even dug through old boxes to find some of my favorite books. These are books I have enjoyed just for the pure pleasure of reading. Here's a list of some of my favorites that I've read over the course of my life. They are listed in no particular order. Some are regular fiction and some are science fiction.

- *Narcissus and Goldmund* by Herman Hesse
- *Islands in the Stream* by Ernest Hemingway
- *The Grapes of Wrath* by John Steinbeck
- *The Count of Monte Cristo* by Alexandre Dumas (the abridged version - it's easier to read)
- *Dune* by Frank Herbert
- *A Boy's Life* by Robert McCammon
- *Mystery* by Peter Straub
- *A Deepness in the Sky* by Vernor Vinge
- *The Lord of the Rings* by J.R.R. Tolkien (I enjoyed the books so much more before the movies came out)
- *The Bourne Identity* by Robert Ludlum
- *The White Dragon* by Anne McCaffrey

This month I'm going to reread three of these books— my choices are *The Count of Monte Cristo*, *A Deepness in the Sky*, and *Dune*.

I'll leave you all of my copies so you can read at your leisure. Enjoy!

February 12 Journal Entry

Today is my birthday - 58 years old. It's a bittersweet birthday knowing that most likely this will be my last. I'd be happy with at least five more birthdays. I'd give anything to be free of this cancer.

When I woke up this morning, I was thinking of all my birthdays. Which ones stand out in my memory? That's an interesting question.

The first birthday I clearly remember is my seventh birthday. This was a memorable one. My mom was in the hospital after giving birth to my youngest brother - he was born on February 9, but they had to stay over for a few days. My birthday party was almost cancelled, but at the last minute my aunt, my mom's sister, came to the rescue and hosted my birthday party at my house. I was so happy that I still had my party. Whenever I see my aunt I always thank her for saving the day.

I remember turning twelve. I got a jean jacket, which was the cool thing you had to have. I was so excited to get it. My mom gave it to me.

Sixteen is memorable, only because I got my driver's license the same day and was officially driving. (Even though I already had a learner's permit).

Twenty-one was great. One of my buddies took me out on the town - it was a Saturday night. We hit all the bars on the mall, and I got to drink for free since it was my twenty first birthday. We had a great time.

Thirty was memorable because I was in Martinique at a resort. Very pretty there - I loved the water. There's great scuba diving there, which was the best part of that trip.

Then I remember all of my birthdays as you were growing up. You made each of them so special.

Forty stands out because we threw a big party and invited a ton of people. I got a lot of gag gifts and that was a lot of fun.

Fifty was a non-event. I remember the weather was really awful and my birthday was on a Tuesday. We just didn't plan that one out very well.

I look forward to a fifty-nine but we shall see how things turn out.

February 19 Journal Entry

One of the nice things about the past few weeks is that I've reconnected with a lot of my old friends and extended family - a combination of me tracking some of them down or them getting in touch with me. When you have cancer, word gets out fast and people find out about it, so a lot of my friends and family have been reaching out to me.

I feel bad that I have not done a better job of keeping in touch with my friends and family over the years. Now it's too late. Some people are okay to talk openly about the cancer, while others completely try and avoid it, so some of my conversations are not like they used to be when I was healthy.

It wouldn't have taken much for me to call, email, or even visit people over the years to keep in touch. I should have done more. Everywhere you go when you travel, you're bound to be in an area where an old friend or relative lives.

I'll never forget, years ago, when I was in Baltimore for a sales conference. I was out walking in the harbor area, which is very popular with lots of shops, restaurants, and bars. As I was walking, I literally bumped into my best friend from junior high. He was out on a date with his girlfriend who eventually became his wife. We chatted a bit, just like old times. The next time I traveled to Washington, DC, we got together with a couple of our other buddies. I'll never forget that time when we all went out to a steakhouse in northern VA. I had another great guys' night out at an awesome steakhouse in DC a few years later. Great thing about keeping in touch with friends from your childhood is they know the real you - you can't hide or fake anything with them. It's refreshing being with friends like that because you can just be yourself.

The phone calls the past couple of weeks have been invigorating - so nice to hear from friends and family. But I do regret that I let a lot of my friendships slide as I grew older. I guess it's because I was busy with my life. Everyone is so busy nowadays. For me it was the usual - busy with work, busy with family, busy with responsibilities, busy with being busy. I feel a sense of loss knowing I missed out on a lot of good times with friends and family.

March 3 Journal Entry

The subject of this entry is suicide. I have been thinking about it because I am exposed now to a lot of people who are terminally ill, yet they remain as happy as they can be, given their situation. They are not giving up - they keep fighting and remain positive. I'm just amazed by the strength of the human spirit in these people.

Why discuss suicide? Because it's been on my mind lately, and it's a worthy discussion when you realize how valuable health and living a long life are for most of us. In my life, I knew three people who committed suicide. I had a very hard time understanding why they did it. I was a casual friend with all three, but I really felt a sense of loss each time it happened. I spent days and weeks after each person died in a mini-depression, because I just could not understand why it happened.

The first person I knew who committed suicide was a young woman - we were both in our twenties. I knew her from a circle of friends. We hung out together a few times. I even went out on a date with her - it was uneventful, just going out to have fun. A month or so after our date, I heard she drove her car over a cliff into a canyon. Crazy! I could not believe it. I didn't know her very well but it really bothered me. What was going on in her life that would cause her to make that choice?

The second person I knew who committed suicide was a co-worker. We both worked at the same company. I was in my mid-thirties, and he was in his mid-twenties. He worked in the professional consulting department, and I was in the sales department, so we did have some overlap in our jobs. He was like a prodigy - extremely bright, and a rising star within the company. I worked with him for three years. We even lived in the same city after we were no longer co-workers. I used to see him on a regular basis at one of the local grocery stores. He was a really nice guy. Well, I found out one day he had committed suicide - he hung himself in his own house. He lived by himself. I was really shaken up. I couldn't stop thinking about why and how this could happen to a guy like him. He was so smart, very successful, and had a beautiful girlfriend. I found out after it happened that he suffered from "night terrors," something I had never been exposed to in my life. I had heard about it before in relation to kids but not adults. Even to this day I am shaken up by his death. Very, very sad.

The last person I knew who committed suicide was another sales guy I knew in the industry. I did some business with him once and he was a real professional - very sharp and good to work with on a deal. He was a tall guy, good-looking, and very charismatic. He was the person everyone would gravitate towards at a party. I don't remember the details of his death. I just heard after it happened that he was gay and for whatever reason it drove him to suicide. Again, another big loss. I just could not believe his problems were so big that he had to kill himself.

Why am I going through all of this? I just want you to be exposed to these situations. We all have tough times, but committing suicide is never the answer. I am reminded of this whenever I am in the hospital and I see other cancer patients battling every single day to beat their cancer and stay alive. These patients know the true value of life. I wish I could have talked to the three people I knew before they committed suicide. They needed medical attention, which I feel could have helped them and prevented what happened.

Michelle, maybe you know someone who committed suicide. Take it to heart - it is never the answer to anyone's problems.

Eight

I had to stop reading Dad's journal for a few minutes. I called Mom to tell her lunch was definitely out for today, but maybe we could still do dinner.

I can't believe Dad wrote this journal after he was diagnosed with cancer. I never saw him writing it. He must have done it at night when no one was around. It feels so weird reading his thoughts now. I wish he were still here.

I remember Dad talking about the person he worked with who committed suicide; it really surprised him. No one I know has committed suicide. It must be hard on the loved ones left behind.

I wish I had more friends now. I should do a better job of keeping in touch with all of my old friends. It's a small world, and even though some of them don't live close to me, we can get together once or twice a year. It's on me; I need to do it.

I didn't know the story about Dad's seventh birthday and how his aunt saved the party. Last year we didn't even celebrate my birthday. What was the point? Dad had just passed away the day before. It was so hard on Mom and me. I know Dad didn't want it to end that way for him, and he tried as best he could to be there for my twenty-fourth birthday. I hope my future birthdays are more enjoyable and memorable than last year.

March 12 Journal Entry

One of the biggest challenges facing your generation and beyond is choosing a career path. It's so confusing now to choose the right job out of college. There are a lot of dynamic forces to choose from when looking at your work career.

- How do you choose the right career for you?
- How do you know what is right for you when you graduate from college?
- What are the best job opportunities for college graduates?
- Money vs. job fulfillment?
- Passion vs. security?
- Challenging vs. comfortable?
- Corporate vs. independent?

I thought it would be best for you to get a direct sales job right out of college. You would learn the following - sales skills, time management, the corporate side of sales, job pressures, prospecting skills, people skills since you deal with a lot of different types of people, and you would be challenged since the quota system is pretty intense.

My plan was to see how you would do after a few years. If it wasn't for you, I would understand and not feel bad that you wanted to change jobs or go a different way with your career. But unfortunately I will most likely not be around when you hit the wall with your current job. These high-pressure corporate sales jobs for entry-level reps are generally short lived - two to three years at the most and then burnout hits. The management landscape is very political, so even if you do great and you're worthy of a promotion into management it is very rare to see someone so young move into sales management.

So what I'm saying to you is that if you want to change jobs or pursue a new career I will not feel bad, and I don't want you to feel obligated to stay in this job for a long time just because I recommended and helped you get on board with this company. In fact, I know how the management team works there, so I would not be surprised if you quit the company sooner than I expected. It's not your fault. I had similar jobs myself when I started out. Your career is a process and a journey.

What I'd like you to think about is - what do you enjoy doing? How can you blend what you're passionate about into a career? The catchphrase lately has been "find your passion" and make it your career. It's just not that easy, but if you look back at history you will see people who were very passionate about their work and became quite successful at it. Steve Jobs and Mark Zuckerberg are two people who come to mind, both working out of their homes on their projects and building them into huge, profitable companies. I don't expect you to have the same results as these two guys, but on a smaller scale you can do exactly the same thing, as long as you identify what it is you want to do in your work life.

But that is the key question. How do you determine what you like to do and turn it into a career? I don't have any easy answers for this. I believe it takes time, thought, introspection, and good old-fashioned research. I think you need to learn more about yourself.

When you graduated from college, I was torn between recommending two career path choices for you. One plan was for you to jump into the work force right out of college and just start doing it. Get valuable work experience, earn some money, build some confidence, and learn what the real world is like in comparison to what they teach you in college. My other thought was for you to take one year off after college and travel the world. This would have given you some interesting experiences, taught you about other cultures, shown you how others live, and deepened your knowledge after you graduated.

When I graduated from college, I worked in our family restaurant for two years and then had to get a corporate (real) job. Once I started working in the corporate world as an account manager (sales rep), my career path was set. This was not my first choice. I had a plan all in place for my life. After I graduated from college with a degree in political science (I almost qualified for a double major in international affairs), I would sign up for the Peace Corps. I had the application in process to go to Ecuador. After my two and half year stint in the Peace Corps, I planned on going to one of the Washington, DC schools, ideally Georgetown, to study for a master's degree in international affairs. After I got my master's degree, I had planned to either go into law school or get a job in the U.S. Foreign Service in the diplomatic corps. It was a grand plan. I had mapped it all out when I was a senior in college.

But unfortunately it never happened. A turn of events with my dad, mom, and my two brothers prevented me from choosing this life path. I had obligations to the family business to help my parents. I was the oldest child so I had responsibilities. Looking back now I realize that if I had chosen the path I had intended for myself, my life could have ended up better and much different, but my parents and brothers would definitely have suffered. Such are the choices and sacrifices we are forced to make in our lifetime.

This was a life decision that changed my life forever. I think we all have life decisions that shape our lives greatly, but at the time we don't realize their significance to our lives. For example, when I quit playing baseball in my junior year of high school, it seemed like a simple choice of not playing baseball that year, but I would never play organized baseball again in my life. That is a huge regret of mine.

As an aside, a great life decision I made was marrying your mom. I waited a few years, but it was worth it. Maybe she doesn't think it was a great decision for her... Just kidding!

If I had known how much my life would change when I didn't go to the Peace Corps like I had planned after college, I would have fought much harder for myself so I could have lived the life I wanted to. This was a pivotal moment for me - it was my time, my life. But the path I wanted to take was not taken. That time in my life would never come back to me.

So my advice to you is to do what you want with your life, especially when you are in your twenties. Try and find out what you enjoy, and what type of work or career inspires you. Can you find job fulfillment along with a good paycheck? Money isn't everything, but you want some security with your compensation.

Challenge yourself - don't settle for a comfortable job or career. You want to stretch yourself and go to your limits. Once you push yourself and get out of your comfort zone, only then will you grow stronger.

Personal development - keep improving yourself, hone your skills, build your knowledge. If your path leads you to starting your own company, then do it and don't be afraid. The best time to take risks is when you're young and single. I say go for it. I have confidence in you because you are smart, and you have a lot of hidden talents - tap into them. But you have to challenge yourself, and don't settle for comfortable. Being comfortable when you're young is a sure path to failure long-term in your life. This is your time, your life.

The path you choose when you're young, after you graduate from college, defines your life without you realizing it. The little steps you take in your twenties are leading you to a final destination. Keep this in mind, because before you know it you'll be thirty, then thirty-five, and then forty. Once you're forty, it is so much harder to change careers and start over again. Plus, when you're in your thirties and forties, you will probably have family responsibilities with children and a husband, so you want to make sure your career path is set.

I know you want to be your own person and not rely on your husband financially, and you are not one to be a stay-at-home mom. Don't shortchange yourself and give in that way - be productive, have your own career. Your mom and I both had our own careers - your self-esteem is so much higher when you have your own life outside of your marriage. You can put your children in daycare - it's not a crime.

Some people study a field in college that they want to get a job in after they graduate, such as computer science, engineering, medicine, law, or the hard sciences.

I think it's more challenging when you get a degree in business like you did, or like I did with political science. The joke for me was that if you wanted a job with your political science degree, you either became a lawyer or a sales rep. You have so many options available to you - maybe you could go back to college and get an MBA or a master's degree in a more specific field or subject.

I still think you should seriously consider taking a year off to travel the world. Visit and live in countries that get you out of your comfort zone, such as Japan, Russia, India, or China. You can visit Europe as well, but try to get off the beaten path and see some of the history of the European countries. Even if you have to make sacrifices to travel abroad for a year, I think it's worth it. Looking back at my life, I wish I had taken more time to travel. The best time to travel is when you're young, before you're married, and before you have kids. You can see what you want to see, and go to the countries you want to visit. Be adventurous while at the same time being safe and smart when you travel.

March 30 Journal Entry

I've been working on a work career lesson list for you since my last entry. I thought it would be helpful to give you some advice as it relates to your career. I have twenty bullet points I put together for you. I firmly believe if you study these points, they will help you be more successful in your life.

My Top 20 Success List

- Freedom to choose your career. You are not locked into anything. It's your life.

- Believe in what you do. Conviction. Choose and do work that is meaningful to you.

- You can accomplish anything if it's important and meaningful to you. What is your purpose in life? What is important to you? Why? What are your goals? Are your goals important to you? Where do you want to be in the future? 5 years? 10 years? 20 years? You have to think forward to move forward.

- Be your own boss. Be accountable to yourself, to your work. Be responsible.

- Respect. Earn it from your customers, your colleagues, your employees.

- Time management. Don't waste your life on social media or watching TV. Be productive. Live in the moment. Focus on priorities that produce results. Don't do busy work to look good. Results are key to success.

- Sales skills. We all need to know how to sell. Study and improve your ability to connect with people. Add value as a salesperson. Listen to what the customer wants.

- Management skills. As a manager, treat your team with respect, help them, add value, listen to them, and challenge them to be better.

- Push back. Be strong and believe in yourself. The customer is not always right - you have to convince them what you know is best for them. Push back strategies apply everywhere. Do it with diplomacy and you will earn respect. Push back to gauge interest. Push back to determine qualifications.

- Get advice from qualified and experienced experts when you need help.

- Do the work. Don't take shortcuts. No "secret" to success. People will try to tell you there is one, but there isn't. Search within, not without.

- Personal development. Adapt and stay current. Hone your skills. Get better as the years go by. Think about what you do and be creative.

- Balance your life. Work, relationships, spouse, kids, physical health, exercise, mental health, hobbies, leisure time, downtime with friends and family.

- Inspiration. Your faith, meditation, quiet time. Listen to music. Travel - see how other people live around the world.

- Stay calm. Control your emotions. Business is business, it's not personal, be a professional.

- Be positive. Nobody wants to do business with or be around negative people. Enjoy your life and career.

- Don't be a follower. Be genuine. Set yourself apart from the crowd.

- Being comfortable equals stagnation. Don't get too comfortable with your life. Keep striving to get better.

- Don't give up. Stick with it. Your personal success is defined by persistence and hard work.

- No regrets! Don't ever regret not doing something in your life, especially when you're young. Control your fear of the unknown and taking risks. If you believe strongly enough you will achieve it.

Nine

I took out a notepad to make a few notes from Dad's journal. This was a lot of info to absorb in one sitting.

I wrote down: *Money vs. Job Fulfillment?*

What is the real appeal of my current job? I think you'd have to say it's money; I earned well last year. If I were somehow able to make quota again this year, then I would make a lot of money. But do I find the job fulfilling? I'd have to say overall, no. I do enjoy it when things are going well. When deals are happening, then everyone is happy, including me. I just don't know if I can do this job for more than a few years. I think burnout would hit me hard and fast.

What is my passion?

Dad writes about finding your passion. What a difficult question. What is my passion? I don't know. I need to start putting some thought into this for the future. I hate my job now. What would I do in the future? What is my ideal job? Lawyer? Teacher? Realtor? Stay in the world of high tech? I don't know, but I need to figure this out going forward.

Push back.

I like this; I need to be stronger. I hated having Vic walk all over me in the meeting yesterday. I should have pushed back in some way.

Stay calm and control your emotions.

Yes, excellent advice for me. I do have a tendency to make everything personal. I can't let my emotions control me. When that happens I am not effective, my mind goes out of control, and I lose focus. Stay calm. Business is business. I am going to work on this starting next week.

No regrets.

This speaks for itself. I can't be afraid of living my life. I don't want to hold back anymore. What do I have to lose?

April 5 Journal Entry

Here are some business books I have read in my life from my early days to recently. Check some of them out - a number of them are very interesting and helpful.

- *Think and Grow Rich* by Napoleon Hill
- *How to Win Friends and Influence People* by Dale Carnegie
- *Outliers* by Malcolm Gladwell
- *The Tipping Point* by Malcolm Gladwell
- *Blink* by Malcolm Gladwell
- *Crush It* by Gary Vaynerchuk
- *Drive: The Surprising Truth About What Motivates Us* by Daniel Pink
- *Flow: The Psychology of Optimal Experience* by Mihaly Csikszentmihalyi
- *Path of Least Resistance* by Robert Fritz
- *Man's Search for Meaning* by Victor Frankl
- *The Power of Myth* by Joseph Campbell
- *Leadership Is an Art* by Max DePree
- *On Becoming a Leader* by Warren Bennis

My top two - *Outliers* and *The Power of Myth*.

April 10 Journal Entry

I want to follow up on two of the bullet points I listed out for you a few days ago.

I remember years ago when I was a sales rep trying to break into sales management, I so desperately wanted to be a sales manager. I felt that I had put in my time, I was ready to lead a team of reps, but for many reasons I didn't get my shot. I was always held back, primarily by politics - I was not an insider. When I didn't get the promotion, I was at a crossroads. I was so angry and upset because I felt I deserved it. I didn't know what to do - should I have quit? Should I have moved to another company to see if I could have gotten a manager position there? It would have been difficult since, up to that point, I had always been a sales rep. My attitude was in the toilet. I was so frustrated.

I remember talking to one of my colleagues at work that I respected and trusted. He said I should have been promoted, but the only thing I could do about it was to become the top sales rep in the company, blow out my numbers, and then they would have to promote me to manager. My colleague was absolutely correct, and I did exactly what he said. I was so motivated. I had a reason to be the best and it was important to me, so I did whatever it took to become one of the top sales reps in the company. The CEO took notice of my performance, and he told the VP of Sales to promote me into a transitional sales manager position halfway through the year. The next year I was promoted to a full regional manager position, and under my lead, my sales team was the number one region in the company for the year. It was very fulfilling and satisfying. How did I do it? There was no magic involved. I just worked hard, was focused, and motivated to succeed - it was personal for me to show everyone that I was a top performer and a good sales manager.

So when you see yourself struggling in the future, ask yourself why you don't have a good reason to succeed.

Find the reason, find your motivation - it's singular to you. Rather than spinning your wheels, you need to tap into your emotions, look into your heart, and find out what drives you. I know when I look back at my life, the times I have done well were when I had purpose and motivation to succeed. It really is that simple sometimes. We over-complicate our lives. We are always looking for complex answers to life's problems, but life is not that complex. If you only take one thing away from this journal, it is this concept - if you're floating through life and just getting by, look within yourself to find out why you don't have a compelling reason to succeed. Find the reason. Be excited about what you want out of your job and your life.

The second bullet point I want to review is the concept of pushing back. I have talked about this many times to co-workers and sales reps I've managed. It's a negotiating tactic that can be used in any type of situation for work or personal reasons. I'll give a few examples -

You walk into a car lot. A salesperson approaches you, you exchange pleasantries, and you tell the salesperson you'd like to take one of his new cars out for a test drive. What does the salesperson do then? Does he just run off, grab the keys, and you both hop into the car? No, the salesperson says, "Okay let's meet in my office so I can get some information from you before we go out." What do you do? If you really want to take a test drive, you agree to go to the office. The salesperson is pushing back in this instance. You, the customer, want something the salesperson can deliver, but before the salesperson agrees to it they want information from you to help them make the sale in the future.

A little boy asks his mother for a Popsicle - the mom says, "Sure, as long as you clean your room first."

A prospective customer wants a free evaluation of your product. Before you agree to it, you have them fill out a detailed profile form to learn more about their project team and who the decision maker is for purchasing the product.

A prospective buyer for a house wants to schedule a showing to see the home with a real estate agent. The agent says, "Yes, but let's meet at my office or coffee shop first for a few minutes before viewing the home."

An employee of yours wants to take a few days off during the busy season. You agree if they put in some extra hours to help before they take the time off.

Your boyfriend asks you to go see a mindless action movie. You agree as long as you get to choose another activity you want to do together.

Very simple - the classic give-and-take, this-for-that. But people lose their confidence in business and especially in sales situations where they don't do this. It requires confidence to push back effectively and diplomatically. You don't want to piss people off. You can blame it on the company - "I'm sorry, my company policy is we can't give out free software evaluations unless you have this form filled out by your manager." "I'm sorry, I can't take you out for a test drive in the car you're interested in until I get some information from you first." "I'm sorry, I can't meet you at the house you want to see until we meet first - it's company policy." So let's say one of the prospective customers says, after one of these statements, that they can't do it or they don't want to do it. What does it tell you? It clearly says they are either not qualified or not really interested in potentially buying your product. They are most likely just wasting your time. Push back to qualify. Push back to determine interest. I always said the best way to see if a potential customer is really interested in your product is to ask them to do something. When they agree with your request, it shows interest, motivation, and potentially a new customer for you.

I believe most of the items on my twenty point success list are self-explanatory. Study them - they will help you in building a successful career.

April 12 Journal Entry

Why worry? Why do people worry so much? I did my fair share of worrying in my life, and what did it get me? Nothing. Absolutely nothing. The first few years of my sales career, I worried and worried myself to no end. I remember tossing and turning in bed night after night worrying about my next paycheck. Would I be able to make quota? Was I going to be able to close the next big deal? I really worried a lot about work when I was younger and as I progressed in my career. I worried about potential job promotions, about getting a bump in salary, territory realignments, getting a new manager, getting fired, competition from other sales reps, new products, support, price increases, company stock valuations, contract and legal issues on bigger deals, and basically any little thing that came up.

Looking back, it was all so meaningless - a complete waste of time, energy, and my life. The funny thing is more than half of the stuff I worried about never happened. They never came to be. I worried about potential bad stuff happening but they never did, and I ended up working myself up into a frenzy over nothing. I really wish I had not wasted my life worrying so much.

I do remember that we had some situations with you, Michelle, when you were a baby. Nothing bad ever happened, but your mom and I were right to worry about your health. Your mom was not the worrier in the family – I was. I take full credit for all of my non-essential worrying. I hope you don't take after me. It would be best if you were more like your mother. She was very calm about issues and didn't hide or shy away from them, but she just had a more levelheaded approach than I did. I wish I could have been more like her.

I strongly believe your health is tied to how you view life. If you're constantly worrying, then it will affect you over time. As I got older, I worried less. I just remember how much I worried about my job performance in my late twenties and into my early thirties. As I got older, I got better in sales, gained more confidence, and this probably more than anything prevented me from worrying so much.

Balance in life is important. You don't want to be obsessing about your job all the time. Of course you want to be successful, but at the same time you don't want to be a workaholic. You need to have time for other parts of your life - family, friends, hobbies, exercise, and leisure time. I do feel I worked too much during my thirties. That decade of my life I was somewhat obsessed with being a top sales rep. I paid the price by putting in too many hours at work. I regret it now because I should have spent more time at home with you. Those early years when you were a baby were a special time. I wish I could relive them again and watch you grow up - from crawling, to walking, to speaking gibberish, to actually talking. I cherish those memories now. I just wish I had spent more time with you then.

Ten

I need to stop worrying, Dad is right. Yes, I am a worrier.

I wrote down: *What does worrying get you? Absolutely nothing!*

I know it's been hard lately with my job, Josh leaving me, and Dad dying last year. But I have to be stronger; I can't let the dark thoughts take over during the night. I need to create more positivity in my life. I can spend more time with Mom and with my friends, and participate in more activities outside of work. I am going to call my old sensei next week and check into getting involved as a teacher for the younger students at my dojo. I should start playing tennis again; I stopped playing this past year. That's another good idea. I also have a friend who has been asking me to join her for a yoga class recently. I should do that, as well. What do I have to lose?

I was already starting to feel better.

May 14 Journal Entry

Yesterday afternoon I was in the hospital cafeteria to kill time between appointments. I had gotten a light snack for myself to eat. It was a little crowded so I sat next to an older lady. I could tell she was in pain. She was holding a tissue tightly in her right hand, and her eyes were very red. She had no food or drink in front of her, and was just staring off into the distance.

I felt sorry for her. Maybe she needed something. "Can I get you something to eat, something to drink? I'd be happy to get it for you," I said.

She looked at me and smiled. I could tell she had been crying a lot recently. "No, I'm alright. Thanks, hon. I just finished lunch. One of the nice boys over there took my tray for me."

I smiled at her and then started eating my food. I didn't look at her so she could have her privacy.

"Why are you here? Is someone in your family sick?" she asked.

"No, no one in my family is sick. I'm here for myself. I have cancer. I'm here for my treatments and to see my doctor," I said.

"Oh, I am so sorry. I am surprised. You are so young and you look so healthy. I am here because of my husband - he had a stroke last night. It doesn't look good. The doctor said he will not make it through the night." Her eyes welled up with tears, and she dabbed both of them with the tissue she held in her hand.

"I am sorry to hear that," I said.

"Yes, it was quite sudden. I haven't been able to talk to him since it happened. The doctor says my husband will not regain consciousness. Both of us are getting up in years and we knew something like this might happen, but even when you kind of expect it and it actually happens, you're still not ready for it," she said.

I took in what she was saying, but said nothing. I kind of gave her a knowing look.

She continued, "What I am most sad about is that I will not be able to say goodbye to him. We've been married for fifty-three years. We've had our good years, and our difficult years, but we've always been there for each other. I just wish I could have let him know one more time how much I loved him - how he was the best thing in my life. I don't even remember what the last thing I said to him last night was. I think I was complaining about the television show he was watching, and then the next minute I saw something was wrong with him. I called 911 immediately. I have not been able to talk to him since last night. The doctor says my husband will not wake up again..." She sighed deeply, got up from the table, and looked me in the eye, "Make sure you give your family and friends the opportunity to say good-bye." She patted me on the shoulder and slowly made her way out of the cafeteria. I haven't seen her since.

June 2 Journal Entry

Yesterday an old friend visited me at the house. I hadn't seen him in twenty-four years. I remember how long because the last time I saw him was a few months before you were born.

We had a huge falling out. He was one of my best friends for many years. We had entered into a partnership buying a house. We were going to renovate it, then sell it for a profit - a traditional fix and flip. Well, it didn't go as smoothly as we thought it would. We ended up having many disagreements on the "fix" part of the equation. I didn't want to spend much money fixing it up. I wanted to keep it simple, get it fixed up quickly, and then sell it for a fast profit while the market was still strong.

My buddy (at the time) had different ideas. He wanted to do a huge remodel, which would have taken at least six to seven months given our resources. We ended up not doing anything. It turned into a bitter legal battle over ownership of the house. I got tired of it over time, and just wanted it done. I didn't want to keep spending money on legal fees, so we came to a settlement. I ended up losing close to $20,000, but I was happy it was resolved. Our friendship ended, and we hadn't talked to each other since. I remember the last time we spoke I said, "Shame on you" for his poor behavior because he was treating me so badly - not what a true friend would have done. I'm sure he had his reasons why he felt I was not doing the right thing.

So yesterday he showed up at my door. Somehow through the grapevine he heard that I had cancer and it was serious. I was angry at first that he would show up in this manner just because I was going to die. I didn't want his sympathy. He told me he was sorry about what happened all those years ago on the house deal. I remember your mom telling me before we bought the house I should not do business with a friend. She said, "If you value his friendship, you should walk away from the deal so you can remain friends." Your mom was so right.

I told my old friend that I was sorry, as well. We didn't have much to say to each other. He told me he had lost his wife recently to a heart attack, and how it was very hard for him to be alone now. He said he knew what I was going through. I thanked him, but I didn't really want to talk to him. Was it wrong for me to feel that way? He stayed for a half hour before he said he had to be somewhere else. I thanked him for coming by, and for thinking of me.

At the door as he was leaving, he told me something I will never forget. "I am truly sorry our friendship ended the way it did. I know we can't resurrect it now, but I just want you to know it was not personal. I had some crazy ideas back then. I regretted how our friendship ended and I still do to this day. I wish I could go back in time, correct my mistake, and we could have remained good friends for the rest of our lives. I'm truly sorry."

He walked down the sidewalk and out of my life again. All afternoon yesterday I thought about what he said. Yes, I was culpable, too. I played a part in the ending of our friendship. I always regretted losing my good friend. I wish we could go back to that time in our lives.

June 19 Journal Entry

I'm having a hard time keeping up with this journal. I know my time is limited, yet I am still procrastinating. How ironic. In general I have been feeling very down lately. There is no hope for me. I know that now. It makes me very sad that the world will keep spinning without me. I will not be here. I don't want to talk to anyone, I don't want to write anything, I don't want to be with anyone. I don't want to die. I am afraid. I wish it would just be over. This waiting is terrifying. I think it might be better to just be hit by a bus and get it over with. I will do my best to keep a good face for you and your mom, but even that is a real challenge.

July 14 Journal Entry

I almost got rid of my last entry, but I feel for posterity that you should have a record of how I felt. The past month I have been really down. I haven't felt good at all. Every time I thought about my situation I got upset. There is no place to hide if you know you're going to die soon. It was best for me to be alone, but at the same time it's hard to be all alone with your thoughts. I listened to music quite a bit - all types, from classical, to classic rock, to alternative. Listening to music took me to different places in my mind so I wouldn't feel so closed-in with all of this hanging over me.

I feel much better now. I guess I have finally accepted my situation, and I realize now there is nothing I can do about it. In some ways it is a relief to accept my reality. I can't run away from it, I can't hide from it. The reality is that I will die soon. This cancer is not going away no matter what I do. We all knew this was the most likely outcome after my diagnosis, so it is no surprise.

Since I have accepted it, I do feel better now. It's sad, but it is what it is. I don't want to waste any more energy getting angry. It's not worth it anymore. I can't change it no matter how hard I try. I am starting to see my life now in a truer focus - only at the end does life become crystal clear.

There are different forces pulling you in your life. You want to be happy. You want security. You want to be successful. You want to be healthy. What made me happy in my life? What gave me joy? I've been thinking about this a lot lately. Our society usually measures success based on money and fame.

What is success? How do you define it? Is it being rich and famous? When a person who has a lot of money or fame dies, all you hear about is how successful this person was in their life, whatever their story was—inventor, business magnate, sports figure, politician, movie star, rock star, artist—but the measure revolves specifically around how much money they made in their life and how famous they were.

What about the regular person who has lived a worthy life? This person worked hard, took care of their family, was responsible, gave back to the community doing charitable work, but they never got rich, and they were not famous. This person was a success, as well, but no one knew about them. Are they any less worthy than the rich, famous person? Of course not.

Does being successful equate to happiness? In some ways I felt it did, but then you have to look at your definition of success.

Was I successful? This is a tough question. I think in a lot of ways my life was a success. I worked hard, I took care of my family, I was a good husband and a loving father, I was honest, and I was always there for family and friends when they needed help.

But what made me happy in life? I would have to say it was the simple things that made me the happiest - those did not require lots of money or fame. I enjoyed times with my family, like having a nice meal, sitting on the backyard deck on a cool summer evening with family or friends, hiking in the mountains, dinner parties with close friends, playing tennis with my daughter, having a coffee with a friend and chatting away the afternoon, sitting on a beach and watching the ocean waves roll in, business lunches with interesting clients...I could go on and on. Looking back, I see it was those moments in time when things just clicked. I wasn't even trying to have fun or be happy, they just happened. If you add up enough of these moments over time then you can look back and feel good about your life.

The experiences during our lives are far more important than the material objects by which we often measure ourselves. If I had more money in my life, how much different would it have turned out? Would I have been happier? I would have probably lived in a much bigger house, and maybe in a more exclusive neighborhood. I could have had a second home in an exotic beach location or a mountain villa in Aspen. I may have driven a more expensive car, or perhaps had two or three cars rather than just the one I had. Maybe my clothes might have been more fashionable, and I might have owned a huge wardrobe for any occasion. I might have divorced my wife after ten years and married a hot, young trophy wife. Maybe my appearance might have been different - I could have gotten a nose job, a tummy tuck, and Botox on a regular basis. Instead of going to the Outer Banks in North Carolina for a summer vacation every year, I would have gone to the South of France a few times a year where I owned a villa. Rather than being the person who cleaned his own house and cut his own grass, I might have had a maid and gardener to take care of these menial tasks for me. Instead of eating out once a week, I could have gone out every night to a four-star restaurant where all the wait staff knew my name. As you can see, I am totally enjoying this example. Just because I was rich, you can't say I would have been happier. We all know rich and famous people who are not happy. Their stories are plastered all over the supermarket tabloids and nowadays all over the Internet.

But here's the dilemma I face when I evaluate my life - what most often made me happy was a feeling of comfort and security that I had in each moment of time. Could I have done more with my life? Been more productive and accomplished more? Could I have made more money or achieved some level of fame? Could I have created something tangible? Started my own company? Written a book? Invented a new product?

Looking back, I do feel that I got too comfortable with my life. Here's the trap I fell into - I'd go to work for my regular eight to five schedule and usually get home

around six. Some nights I'd try to go the gym if I didn't
go in the morning before work. I was often tired from
a long day of work, so I'd just kind of take it easy at
night, have dinner, hang out with the family, watch TV
(sports, movie, or a lousy show), spend time alone with
your mom, and then go to sleep. Weekends consisted
of chores around the house, yard work, hanging out,
maybe playing golf if the weather was good, going out
to dinner with friends, more TV (especially sports on
weekends), going to parties, spending some time out-
doors, and by the end of the weekend I'd be exhausted.
Then boom, Monday morning started things all over
again.

What happened is over time I lost my sense of hunger.
Basically I got fat and happy. Now I see that I was just
on autopilot - the routine of life consumed me, same
as it ever was. Routine is comfortable. We get used
to a schedule and we feel secure - security in not making any changes, not trying anything new, sticking with
what we know and are comfortable with - the familiar.
In some ways this is a good thing, but it also can be a
curse.

I know now that I never really pushed myself to my
limits fully during my life. I remember when I played
sports or exercised really hard there were always points
when I wanted to quit, and my body was telling me I was
tired. But then my mind took control, I pushed myself
further, and I found that second or third wind. The

mental discipline had won out over my physical fatigue, I ended up having a great workout, and when I finished I was so proud of myself. I stayed with it, hung tough, and fought through the physical pain I was feeling. I am sure you have experienced this as well with your workouts, especially during your intense karate days.

I think I could have applied the same formula to my work career based on what I was able to achieve. Instead of watching TV, I could have been more productive. Instead of surfing the Internet late at night for leisure, I should have been working on projects for myself. Instead of staying at the same company for too many years because it was secure and comfortable, I might have gone out on my own and started a company. I could have done so much more with my life if I just had pushed myself harder.

So my advice to you, Michelle, is to not get too comfortable with your life or stop striving to get better. Security and familiarity can hold you back - be wary of those feelings when you get them. Dream big, create challenging goals, and don't limit yourself like I did. It's not for the money, but to reach your full potential as a human being - as Michelle. Express yourself by pushing forward to fulfill your dreams. The key point here is they need to be your dreams and goals that are important to you and excite you. The enthusiasm you have for where you want to go and who you want to be will give you that second and third wind to allow you to realize your dreams. You have amazing talents. You can do anything you want in this world, but you have to dream it first, and be excited about what you want. Only you can challenge yourself to become a better person. Don't waste your life away. I know you can do it.

Eleven

I cried reading the last entry. Dad knew he was going to die. I felt so bad now knowing what he was going through. He was so strong at the end when I was with him. He put on a good face for all of us.

What he wrote about getting trapped in your routine and being comfortable was very powerful. Even though I've only been working a few years out of college, I see that I've already fallen into a routine with my life. I live comfortably and I am not pushing myself, just like Dad said. I need to change this. I don't want my life to go by without pushing myself to my full potential. I'm twenty-five now: the same age Dad was when he had to take a different life path than what he wanted. Nothing is holding me back. I can do anything I want with my life. I can't let Dad down. I need to live my life; I mean really live it. Don't be afraid, and don't make excuses for myself.

I don't want to quit my job until I make quota. I don't want to be a quitter. I am going to do it; I'll make quota and show those guys. I don't want to regret thirty years from now that I took the easy path.

August 6 Journal Entry

I have been having very vivid dreams lately – you were in a few of them. Last night I had a weird one. I woke up right after it to write it down so I wouldn't forget.

I was on a cruise ship of some kind. I felt really strange because I've never been on a cruise before. I'd rather sit on a beach while on vacation than be cooped up in a huge floating hotel on water. So I was on this huge ship out in the middle of the ocean, but I was all by myself on the top deck standing by the ship's railing, looking out towards the black sea. It was nighttime, and I could see a million stars in the sky. It was breathtaking - the Milky Way was bright as day. I heard people singing and laughing on the lower decks. I found it odd that you and your mom were not with me as I would never go on a vacation like this by myself.

My cell phone rang and I looked at the display - *"Home."* I clicked to answer the call, "Sweetheart, don't leave us. How can you leave us behind?" your mom said before I could even say hello. She sounded frantic. Her voice was very different.

"I don't know why I'm here. I didn't want to go on this cruise. I want to be home with you and Michelle," I said.

"James, I love you. Don't leave, we need you here back home. I can't do this alone," your mom said. The phone connection was not great. There was a lot of static on the line.

"Kayla, I can barely hear you. I don't want to be here, you know that I hate cruises. I don't want to leave you. When we get to the next port, I'll try to get a flight back home as soon as possible. I'll do the best I can to get back to you. I love you Kiki."

"JP, just don't leave us. I can't go on without you. Wait! Michelle wants to talk to you." I could hear her crying as she handed the phone to you.

"Daddy! I love you. Come back to us. Mom and I need you," you said.

"Meeshy, I will come back. I promise you. Remember - even if I'm gone, I'll always be with you."

The phone went dead. I looked at the display - it was dark, all the power was gone. I threw the phone into the ocean. What a piece of junk. I needed to find the captain of this ship, but where could he be? I walked to the front of the ship. There was a light on in a cabin ahead, and a bunch of antennas and wires surrounded it.

I knocked on the door. "Come in, I was expecting you," a voice said. I opened the door and immediately smelled the scent of a honeysuckle bush. I loved that smell. It reminded me of my childhood. I slowly walked into the room. There was a Persian carpet on the floor - a very nice blue one with an elaborate design around the border. It looked very similar to one we had at my home when I was a kid. My dad always had a few Persian carpets in our house when I grew up. There was a black reclining chair set off to the side of the carpet. The voice said, "Please, sit down. I am very busy now but I have time to chat with you for a few minutes." The voice had a warm and inviting tone that was very soothing to the ear. I couldn't tell where the voice was coming from. It just kind of filled the room.

I remained standing. "Where are you? I can't see you," I said.

"I am here. I am always here."

"My name is James Parker. I need to get off this ship. Can you help me?"

"Yes, James, I know who you are. I am sorry to tell you that this is your time - you do belong here." I tried hard to get a sense of where the person was in the room. It was odd - I couldn't tell if the voice was that of a man or a woman. It had such a richness to it, and the sound had a hypnotizing effect on me.

"Are you the captain of the ship? Are you in charge here?" I asked.

"Interesting. Yes, you could say that. I'm sorry James, but what do you want? I am kind of busy. How can I help you?" the voice said.

"I need to get back home. I don't know how I got here, but I would never go on a cruise without my wife and daughter. I don't like being alone. In fact, I'm getting kind of scared being here on this ship. I need to get off at the next port and take a flight back home to my family. Can you help me?"

"We have reached our destination. This ship will never go to port again. You are where you are because this is your time, your life."

"This must be a mistake. It can't be my time yet. I want my life. Please, I have so much to do back home. I have responsibilities. My family needs me."

"Sit in the chair, James." Before I could even think about it, I sat down in the chair. The voice had a power to it that I didn't understand. The chair was comfortable, and I leaned back into it. I felt good sitting there. I was looking at a blank wall.

"James, open your eyes, open your mind, open your heart." The blank wall in front of me changed into a blue sky with clouds floating by. I could feel the wind on my face.

"What is happening?" I asked.

"You are safe with me. Come, be one with me," the voice said.

Suddenly the room disappeared. I was no longer sitting in the comfortable chair. I was flying through the clouds. I was flying. I could feel my body soaring through the clouds. I loved it, but I kept thinking, *"I need to go home. Kayla and Michelle need me. I love them. They are my life."*

The voice said, "This is your home now. You are here."

I yelled, "No! I am not ready yet. Please!"

Then I fell from the sky. I couldn't fly anymore. I was going down, and I couldn't see anything because I was in the clouds. I kept falling. I was scared and my heart was pounding like a hammer through my chest. I descended faster and closed my eyes. It seemed like an eternity as I fell below the clouds. I opened my eyes - the deep blue ocean was just in front of me, and my body splashed into the warm water. I couldn't swim. I just sank deeper and deeper into the water. Somehow I could still breathe. It grew darker the farther I sank. I tried to talk but couldn't. I wanted to say something to the person who was in the room with me, but they were gone.

Then the dream ended. That was all I could remember.

I've never had a dream like this before in my life. It was so vivid, so powerful. I actually felt like I was there.

August 15 Journal Entry

I've spent most of today looking at pictures of you. Great memories - bittersweet reliving them. I wanted to share with you my favorite memories of you.

The day you were born. It was right after your birth. The doctor placed you on a tray just before they washed you up. I walked over to you and said, "Hi baby girl." You heard my voice and recognized it. You turned your head towards me a bit and looked right at me with your beautiful eyes. You were just minutes old, yet you knew I was your father.

You were about eighteen months old. We were in the kitchen - you, me, and your mom. You wanted something, but we didn't give it to you. You started crying like anything. You cried so much that you stopped breathing. Your face started to turn blue, so your mom called 911. I picked you up, turning your face to the floor. You still weren't breathing, so I turned you over and started blowing air in your face. You finally started breathing again. The whole event didn't last that long, but it felt like forever for your mom and I. I took you upstairs to put you in your crib to give you a sense of comfort and security. You weren't crying now, just very quiet. In a few minutes we heard the sirens - a fire truck, an ambulance, and a police car were all in front of our house. I brought you back downstairs and sat on the couch in the front room with you on my lap. Bang, bang, bang - the firefighters knocked on the door. Your mom opened the door, and two firefighters, a paramedic, and a police officer all came into the house. You sat there on my lap like nothing had happened, calm as a cucumber as all these strangers with their heavy gear on entered our house. Your mom and I felt foolish about calling 911 because you were totally fine now. The paramedic still checked you out, and said you were A-OK. He said kids sometimes can't catch their breath if they cry too much, but there was nothing to worry about because they will unconsciously start breathing again. We asked him if this might happen again, and he told us 'yes' there was a good chance, but not to worry about it. From that time forward, until you were about four years old, we were terrified every time you started crying intensely. We didn't even feel comfortable leaving you with a babysitter. You never had an incident at daycare, which was a huge relief for us.

One of my favorite memories is when you were about the same age or so - about eighteen months. It was just you and I in the house, and we were listening to music together - *Queen's Greatest Hits.* "Don't Stop Me Now" started playing. I picked you up in my arms and held you close as we danced together listening to Freddie Mercury sing his heart out. I turned the music up really loud and sang along with Freddie. You giggled, we laughed together, smiled at each other, and shared a great moment. Since that time, whenever I hear that song I always think of you and I dancing together. I swung you around all over the kitchen. It was so much fun. I wish you could remember it the same way I do.

Your first day of school was a lot of fun. Your mom cried when you went to school. I was so proud of you with your backpack on, waiting in line with the other kids for the teacher to open the door to let you in. You might even remember this day. I got a great picture of you in front of the school. You had the happiest smile on your face.

We were in Cancun for a family vacation when you were probably around eight years old. You were intently scouring the beach for seashells. You were so disappointed because you couldn't find any after spending all afternoon going up and down the beach in front of our hotel. A really good storm blew in, and it rained like anything that night. But the next day it was sunny and warm in the afternoon. You hit the jackpot on the beach. You were picking up seashells right and left. I remember clearly how you had enlisted a lot of the other guests at the hotel to help you in your treasure hunting. That night, back at the hotel, you laid out all of your seashells on two towels on the floor. You were so proud of your collection. We had to take quite a few of those seashells back home in our suitcases. Yes, I do remember that trip.

You had a sleepover party for your birthday when you were thirteen years old - the first time we let you have a big sleepover. You invited seven to eight girls, and we took you all out to dinner, then back to our house. You had so much fun. You giggled with all of your girlfriends all night and watched a scary movie. One of the girls didn't want to stay any more so I had to call her dad at one o'clock in the morning to come pick her up. The rest of you stayed up until four o'clock in the morning. After that, I was not a fan of big sleepovers.

Our Disney trip to Orlando. Epcot was my favorite spot. It was a great family evening, the three of us together. We walked through all the different countries, and ate dinner at a nice Chinese restaurant. We took some amazing family pictures with the sunset behind us. You did the Meeshy dance for us - I got it on video. You were so happy. It was so much fun.

I have so many memories of your karate days—tournaments, competitions, and the tests for all of your belts over the years. What I remember most is not the tournament you won when you were sixteen, but the one you lost when you were fourteen. You competed well, but you lost in the championship match. You gave it everything you had even when you knew you were overmatched. I was so proud of you that day. That was one of the first times I saw how much courage and perseverance you have within yourself. I think you even surprised yourself by how well you did in the match.

I truly believe losing that championship match drove you to win the tournament when you were sixteen.

Of course I was proud of you when you graduated from high school and college. Your mom and I expected nothing less. I remember both graduations, and how beautiful and proud you looked with your whole future ahead of you.

I remember the one boyfriend you dated who was scared of me after I gave him a big speech the first time he took you out. I think that was the only time he ever came to our house to pick you up. You always asked me what I told him. Well, this is what I said - I told him I had a lot of friends who were ex-Navy SEALs and they knew how to inflict pain on people without leaving any marks or scars. He took it hook, line, and sinker. I always had a little fun with your dates when they came to the house. I guess I was testing them to see what kind of mettle they had and if they were worthy of going out with you. One of the perks of having a beautiful daughter - as a dad you were expected to give all the suitors a hard time.

The day you bought your condo, I remember how you asked me to go to the closing with you to sign all of the papers. I said I wouldn't go because you needed to do it on your own. You were quite surprised, but afterwards I think you appreciated me letting you do it on your own. I was very proud of you buying your own place before you were twenty-five years old.

I don't want to talk much about what has happened this year. It has been a very hard time for you and your mom. When I'm gone, check in on her every now and then. She's younger than me, so I fully support her if she ever remarries. Let her know that when the time comes. I wrote a long letter for her as well for after I'm gone, and in it I explained how she should remarry if she ever meets another man worthy of marrying her.

I commend you on how strong and brave you've been in dealing with the doctors, medical staff, and myself included. You are a very special girl. I am very proud you are my daughter. Enough said here.

August 17 Journal Entry

I would give anything I have right now to be on the beach again - to live on a Caribbean island for a year. It would have been awesome to wear shorts, flip-flops, and a tank top every day. I miss the ocean. I always loved the water and seeing the waves come in, one after the other, never ending, each different than the one before. The beach engages all of your senses - you see the water, the sky, the clouds, the birds, smell the salt water, the sand, the rain, hear the ocean, the waves crashing into the sand, the sounds of the birds, the kids playing in the sand, and the old timers snoring in their chairs on the beach.

If I can list one more regret in my life it's that I wish for at least a year or two I had lived right by the ocean in a little house. Heck, I would have been happy to live in a thatched hut as long as I could see the ocean from my kitchen table. I just loved being on the beach.

I have a lot of memories of family vacations from when I was a kid growing up. We used to go to Virginia Beach. We camped out at Seashore State Park on the Chesapeake Bay. I remember going out crabbing with my brothers and cousins. We had our little rubber rafts, our long rope with a rock at the end and a few chicken necks tied up in the middle of the rope, our nets for catching the crabs, and a little Styrofoam cooler in the raft to keep the crabs after we caught them. I remember one of my cousins always wore his tennis shoes in the water because he hated having the crabs nip at his feet. We'd throw the rope in the water with the rock weighing it down, and slowly pull the rope towards the raft while the other person would net the crabs that were hanging on the chicken necks. We had a great system down, and we caught a lot of beautiful Chesapeake blue crabs that way. We'd take our catch back to the campsite. I remember my dad collecting all the crabs and trying to get them into the pot for cooking. We always had a few crabs escape. We'd all yell and scream as we tried to evade them while my dad did his best to scoop them up and back into the pot.

I remember once we got the tail end of a hurricane while we were there. It rained and rained for a few days. We watched the young, crazy guys surfing the huge waves - they were awesome. It rained so much that we had to watch a movie in the theatre since it was so boring hanging out in the tents in the rain. We all saw *Romeo and Juliet* as a family. I must have been twelve or thirteen when I saw it, and I do remember I cried (spoiler alert) when Romeo and Juliet died. As an adult, it's amazing what you remember of your childhood days. I remember we didn't have much money growing up, so those vacations at Virginia Beach were glorious times.

I remember our time - you, me, and your mom - together on our family vacations - from Cancun, to La Jolla, Sedona, Victoria, Montreal, Turks and Caicos, India, the Florida Beaches, the Outer Banks, to the Thailand Beaches, and Hawaii. We did get to visit a lot of beaches together as a family. I can't complain. I hope you have good memories of your family vacation days like I have from my days at Virginia Beach. I think that's enough writing about beaches.

August 18 Journal Entry

I See You, Michelle

I see you—I am with you. I see you—I love you.

I see you—I am proud of you. I see you—I miss you.

I see you—happy. I see you—standing tall and strong.

I see you—beautiful. I see you—successful.

I see you—smiling. I see you—laughing.

I see you—my daughter. I see you—my big girl.

I see you—with your husband. I see you—with your children.

I see you—in your home. I see you—missing me.

I see you—being you. I see you—raising your children.

I see you—fulfilled. I see you—working hard.

I see you—traveling. I see you—playing tennis.

I see you—teaching your kids karate. I see you—proud.

I see you—respected. I see you—important.

I see you—loving your family. I see you—loved.

I see you—I love you. I see you—I am with you.

August 19 Journal Entry

This most likely will be last entry. I have said all I have to say to you given how much time I have left. I wrote a lot more than I expected to write to you. I truly hope what I have said will be of some value to you. At least I have left something tangible behind for you. It's not *War and Peace*, but I am proud of what I did write these past few months. I just wish I had more time.

This is what it all comes down to - how much time we all have here on Earth together. It is so fleeting. Fifty-eight years is nothing. I am just a speck of sand when you look at the history of the planet. The world will go on without me. Only a few people will take notice. You and your mother will be most affected, the rest of my family, some friends, and that's about it. You'll remember me on the anniversary of my passing and maybe my birthday. You'll look at pictures of me, some videos, and maybe you'll reread what I have written for you. I'll just become a memory. Then one day you and Kayla will be gone as well. This is the nature of our life - it always comes to an end. Sadly we don't get to live forever. We don't even all get to live as long as we want to live. I would have been very happy to live to eighty years - that is a nice round number. Having an extra twenty-two years from this point in my life would have been amazing. I could have seen you grow into your adult years, and maybe been able to bounce a grand-child on my knee. Teach him or her how to throw a baseball, play cards, do a puzzle, and enjoy a family beach vacation with all of us together. Now that would have been heaven to me.

I love you, Michelle. I could not have asked for a better, more loving daughter than you. I have been proud of you every day of your life. I remember when you were young - six or seven years old - how you used to say, "Daddy, I love you," and I would say "I love you, too." Then you would say, "You are the best daddy in the history of daddies." I think you always said this after I got you some ice cream or you got what you wanted. So now I get to say, "Michelle, you are the greatest daughter in the history of daughters. I love you. Even when I'm gone, I will always be with you." That felt good. Stay strong, be true to yourself, push yourself to be a better person, don't get too comfortable with your life, and keep striving to get better. Enjoy life! Don't worry. Goodbye Michelle.

James Parker

Michelle Parker's Dad

Kayla Kumar's Husband

Twelve

I had dinner with Mom tonight. We had a good time together: a simple celebration for my birthday. I didn't talk much about Dad's journal. I planned on reading it again tomorrow. Dad wrote a long letter to Mom before he died, and she said she reads it whenever she misses him. I asked Mom if she felt that Dad lived a happy life. She thought so, but she always felt like he didn't truly enjoy the work he did. She felt he did it because he needed to make money for the family. Mom earned well as a lawyer, but Dad wanted to carry his weight. He was not one to stay at home and be "Mr. Mom."

I was in bed now, and it was close to midnight. I thought of Dad: I loved him, he was my rock, and he was always there for me. I was so happy to have his journal now. I would cherish it for the rest of my life. A warmth coursed through my body. I felt happy. It was a good feeling.

I closed my eyes and saw Dad in my mind. We were sitting on the beach together looking out at the blue water. We both sat in silence staring at the sunset over the water. The colors were glorious–red, purple, blue, yellow, orange, pink—a kaleidoscope of colors. Dad looked at me after the sun went down below the horizon; he was smiling and said, "Michelle, I will always be with you." I drifted off to a peaceful sleep.

Epilogue

Four Months Later

My cell phone alarm went off. It was morning already. I rolled over in my bed; it was so comfortable. I was really impressed with the mattress: firm, but not too firm. I hate squishy soft mattresses. I wanted to look outside. I got up from the bed, pulled the curtains back, and opened the glass sliding door. The salty air hit me first. It had rained the night before, and you could feel the humidity. I took in the view. The Caribbean Sea was a sight to behold: so blue, so rich in color. I made it. I was in Cancun. I saw it in my mind, I worked for this, and I made it happen. Yes! I felt a rush of blood course through my body.

I sat down on the little patio chair on the balcony. I was pretty high up on the sixth floor of the hotel; it was the top floor. I wanted to wake up a little early to take in the morning view. I slept so well the night before. Lately I had been sleeping with no problems. I hadn't woken up in the middle of the night for a couple of months now.

Mom and I flew into Cancun early yesterday afternoon so we had time to settle in, have a nice dinner, and get to bed. We were meeting for breakfast in an hour.

Today was the second day of January. I had planned this trip a few days after my birthday in August. I thought Cancun was a lot better than West Palm Beach. After reading my dad's letter, I really didn't know what to do. It was all so confusing. I hated my job, but I didn't want to quit: at least not yet.

I made a few changes with my life. I got back into karate and started teaching at my old dojo on Saturdays. My sensei was so happy to see me get involved with her dojo again. And I started taking hot yoga classes three to four times a week. I love the yoga classes; it has truly been a cleansing experience for me physically and mentally. I started playing tennis again a little bit. I found a new tennis partner to play with named Steve. Tennis has evolved into us seeing each other a few times socially. Steve is nice, but I am taking it slow, because I am not ready for a serious relationship yet.

I was happy for Mom, also. She went back to work in September at her old law firm. After my birthday, Mom and I began a "girl's night" every week on Thursdays. We meet at a restaurant for dinner, and sometimes some of our friends join us.

I made a vow to myself that I would finish the year at my job and do whatever it took to make quota. I didn't want to get fired, or quit if I was not going to make quota. It wasn't easy, but it was simple. I just worked much harder than I was working before. The key difference now was that I was motivated. I had a reason; it was important for me to make quota. I was on a quest. It was as if my life depended on it. I planned to go out in style. The only way to do that was to stick it to Vic and Colin by making my numbers, so that is exactly what I did. By the third week of December I was at 110% for the year, and I had a nice buffer going into the last week of the year. My final number ended up at 117% for the year.

I never felt so good in my life before. I did it. I had a good pipeline in the summer and was able to pull all my deals in. I was a closing machine. My confidence was at an all time high going into the fourth quarter, and I totally nailed it the last two months of the year.

On December 31, I proudly went into Colin's office at the end of the day and submitted my letter of resignation. He was stunned that I was quitting. At first he thought it was a practical joke or something. I told him I had better things to do with my life. He had me wait a few minutes while he got Vic on the phone.

Colin said Vic wanted to talk to me but I refused. Colin put Vic on speakerphone, and Vic did his best song and dance. He tried hard, and he didn't even say the "F" word once because he knew how much I hated it. I said no, my decision was final, I was resigning, and I gave them a week's notice. Colin took the phone off speaker, listened to Vic, and then hung up the phone.

"So sorry you feel this way, Michelle. Vic feels its best that we make today your last day," Colin said.

"I understand. I have my personal items already boxed up. I'll just go to my desk to get it," I said.

I knew exactly how these guys operated. They would never let me hang around for a week or two after I quit. They wanted me out, pronto: especially one of their top performers who quit on them. I put my identification badge and key card on Colin's desk. I got up to leave, and there was a big fat security guard waiting at Colin's door.

"I'm sorry Miss, but I have to escort you out of the building. Is there anything I can get for you?" the guard said.

I was surprised by his kindness. "It's a good thing you're being nice to me."

"Excuse me?" He had a questioning look on his face.

"No, it's nothing. Just an inside joke."

The guard walked by my side to my desk. I had a big smile on my face, and my head was held up high.

Hillary caught me in the hall. She was out of breath from running to catch up with the security guard and me. "What's going on? Are you being fired? You made quota; you can't be fired."

"No, I quit. This has been my plan since Vic cussed me out in that meeting back in August. I am too good for this company." I said.

I made it to my desk and picked up the box with all of my stuff. "Keep in touch, Hillary. I'm flying to Cancun tomorrow with my mom. We'll be there for a week."

"Cancun? Nice, looks like somebody had this all planned out."

She gave me a big hug, and I hugged her back. "You'll be the one person I'll miss here."

"What about Antonio?" Hillary winked at me.

"Maybe when I get back from Cancun, who knows? I no longer work here. I can fish off this company pier now."

I came back to reality, sitting on the balcony looking out at the Caribbean. That was a great day when I quit my job. I had planned that out for a while. I knew they would escort me out of the building: a very predictable bunch.

In December, I started making plans for my future. I knew I would make quota, so I started networking to check out other job options. I connected with two companies, went through the interview process, and at the end of the interviews I had two job offers waiting for me. I told them I couldn't quit until the end of December, and that I had my Cancun trip with my mom. Both companies understood, and they still really want to hire me. It feels good to be wanted.

I also looked into taking the next LSAT for law school; the next one is in February. I was seriously considering this option because I could take the spring and summer off, and then start law school in the fall.

I also thought about just taking the entire year off to travel. I had enough money saved up, so I could do it.

So what do I do with my life? What path do I choose? I didn't have to decide right this minute. I had given myself some time to think things over on this trip with Mom. I will choose what I want to do.

I planned on rereading Dad's journal to me on this trip. He had a lot of good ideas that I used to help me focus over the last half of the year to reach my quota.

Now I wanted to spend a quality week with Mom. We would have fun.

I looked out at the ocean. I felt at peace, and a sense of calmness. I was one with myself.

"Dad, you're right. This is my time, my life."

The End

About the Author

Mario Jannatpour was born in Washington, DC. He moved to Boulder, Colorado as a teenager with his dad, mom, and two brothers. Mario graduated from the University of Colorado with a degree in political science. He currently lives in the Boulder area.

Made in the USA
Lexington, KY
15 April 2015